INSTRUCTOR'S MANUAL

World Mythology

AN ANTHOLOGY OF THE GREAT MYTHS AND EPICS

World Mythology

AN ANTHOLOGY OF THE GREAT MYTHS AND EPICS

THIRD EDITION

Donna Rosenberg

NTC *Publishing Group*
a division of NTC/CONTEMPORARY PUBLISHING GROUP
Lincolnwood, Illinois USA

Photo Credits:
Page 1: Wolfgang Kaehler/Corbis; **page 19:** Christie's Images.

Sponsoring Editor: Marisa L. L'Heureux
Product Manager: Judy Rudnick
Art Director: Ophelia Chambliss
Production Coordinator: Denise Duffy-Fieldman
Cover illustration: Tony Stone Images

ISBN: 0-8442-5965-9 (hardbound student text)
ISBN: 0-8442-5966-7 (softbound student text)
ISBN: 0-8442-5974-8 (instructor's manual)

890 VP 0987654321

Contents

PART 1

Introduction

Revised for use with the third edition of *World Mythology,* this Instructor's Manual is designed to facilitate your use of the *World Mythology* student's text. The following section will give you an overview of the contents of this Manual and of the philosophy that shapes the instructional format of *World Mythology.*

Part One of this Manual begins with the criteria for choosing the selections and for creating the versions of the myths provided in the text. It includes teaching objectives and suggestions for using *World Mythology* in the classroom, as well as a table of contents arranged by type of myth to assist you in using *World Mythology* as a course of comparative mythology.

Part One also includes a section that explains how to use the instructional format of *World Mythology* and this Manual to enhance your students' literary experience through reading and discussion and through a variety of creative thinking and writing activities.

Part Two of this Manual is devoted to a detailed treatment of each of the selections in *World Mythology.* It supplies background information that has not been included in the student's text, discusses the questions that are located at the end of the student's text, and provides thought-provoking material in the form of supplementary questions, concepts, and suggestions.

CHOICE OF SELECTIONS IN WORLD MYTHOLOGY

World Mythology is a gold mine for teachers because it gathers together in one book the greatest and most interesting myths from around the world. These can be used by a broad range of readers in a variety of ways, thus meeting the individual needs of both teachers and students. *World Mythology* includes the major creation, fertility, and hero myths from the ancient Middle East, ancient Greece and Rome, the Far East and Pacific Islands, the British Isles, Northern Europe, Africa, and the Americas. It presents these myths as fine literature rather than as long summaries and introduces each of them with a detailed commentary that highlights their historical background, their appeal and value, and their literary style.

World Mythology has been designed to meet four major goals. First, the inclusion of comparable myths from the major world cultures reveals that human beings are remarkably alike in their principal values and concerns through time and across space. Using *World Mythology,* it is possible to study the creation, fertility, or hero myths from a variety of cultures and to examine how the values expressed in each myth represent the individual culture and how each myth unites with myths from other cultures to reveal common values.

Second, these myths introduce the reader to a variety of fine stories, including selections from cultures that are not well known in our own culture. The Greek and Roman myths are the most available and popular myths in Western culture, followed by the Norse myths. One must find individual collections of myths organized by individual cultures in order to read myths from the Middle East, the Orient, the Pacific Islands, Africa, and the Americas. Consequently, *World Mythology* is unique in its selection of myths. It permits teachers and students to read both *The Iliad* and *Gassire's Lute,* both "Pyramus and Thisbe" and "Quetzalcoatl." Within the covers of *World Mythology* the reader will find many small gems tucked among the greatest stories in the world.

Third, *World Mythology* makes available to a broad range of students the world's greatest myths in a form that has preserved their literary appeal. Each myth contains the principal plot, the characterization of major characters through authentic dialogue, and the literary style of the original, so that it can be taught on a serious intellectual level as a work of literature. Ordinarily, students have no access to the world's greatest epics until they enter college. There, unfortunately, the elaborate language and style, the complexity of the plot, and the press of time lead even the better students to rely upon the summaries in Cliffs Notes rather than to experience the authentic, unabridged translation. I have therefore designed these versions to give students the feeling of the authentic works which no summary can convey. If students read no further than this book, they will have experienced the unique qualities inherent in Homer, Virgil, and the poets of *Gilgamesh, Beowulf,* and *The Ramayana.* It has been my experience that many students will be motivated by these versions to read the longer, unabridged translations with understanding and enthusiasm and may even choose to study a particular foreign language in order to read one of these myths in the original language.

Finally, *World Mythology* enables teachers from a variety of academic disciplines to explore its riches. Besides providing a stimulating literature program, the myths coordinate well with the study of ancient and medieval history, archaeology, psychology, sociology, anthropology, and religion. They also supplement programs in art and in music, which often include mythological subjects.

The myths told in *World Mythology* will appeal to readers of all ages and academic abilities, for the stories make good listening as well as good reading. They emphasize action and vigorous conversation, with literary style conveyed through modern, vivid, yet appropriate vocabulary. Open-ended questions about each myth lead both listeners and readers to consider a variety of interpretations. These questions emphasize the ability to use facts and implications as a basis for independent and creative thinking. However, the exciting plots can be used to teach more rudimentary reading comprehension skills as well.

STANDARDS OF COMPOSITION

The need to create one volume of manageable length has necessitated the abridgment of many of the longer myths and epics. I have worked from multiple authentic translations of each myth in order to fashion the version presented in the student text. In each case, my goal has been to preserve as much of the literary quality of the original myth as possible, without interpolation and distortion. For example, I have been careful not to make Virgil sound like Homer, and I have summarized material only where it has been necessary to make parts of a myth flow as a coherent whole. In each instance, the major sections of each myth are presented in their entirety as they read in any fine translation of the original.

I was helped in this process by the fact that many of the myths and epics originated in the oral tradition, where an elaborate system of repetition existed within the myth itself to aid the listener in remembering the complex story. With as many as one third of the lines in Homer, for example, repeated once and often twice throughout the epic, it was easier than one might think to pare down even the greatest myths. Other omissions involve incidents of secondary importance, such as the adventures of subsidiary heroes in the Trojan War and the inclusion of peripheral myths in *The Iliad*, the tales about subsidiary characters in *Sigurd the Volsung*, the minstrel's tales in *Beowulf*, the adventures of subsidiary knights in *King Arthur*, and secondary battles in *The Ramayana* and *Kotan Utunnai*. The Notes section at the back of the student text provides detailed information about any abridgments.

TEACHING OBJECTIVES FOR WORLD MYTHOLOGY

World Mythology meets three primary objectives:

1. *To Foster an Enjoyment of Literature.* Particularly today, when students are inundated with television programs, videos, and cheap novels, it is important that the primary objective in studying mythology should be the enjoyment

of fine literature. No matter what else a student learns, if he or she does not enjoy the experience of reading and feel that it has been of personal value, the value of the total experience will be of little lasting merit. The study of myths introduces students to many of the greatest adventure stories in the world, stories that have been enjoyed for hundreds of years because they are both imaginative and relevant to each individual's life experiences. Class discussions should help students relate these myths to themselves and to others, making the students more perceptive in terms of their own attitudes and behavior and more understanding of the attitudes and behavior of others.

Fostering an enjoyment of literature can also improve students' reading comprehension. *World Mythology* motivates reading because each myth is an exciting story. *World Mythology* helps students develop the ability to remember the sequence of principal events and the important details of plot, and also the ability to discern both cause-and-effect relationships and implied character motivation. In addition, reading *World Mythology* helps students develop the ability to discern the specific characteristics that make a particular myth reflect the values of its culture and the ability to discern both similarities and differences between one creation myth and another, one fertility myth and another, one hero myth and another, and one character and another. Students also learn to use stated and implied factors to form independent and creative judgments, to be able to compare different versions of a particular myth and evaluate them in terms of their literary quality, to be able to express thoughts effectively both orally and in writing, and to be able to create an original creation, fertility, or hero myth using the values and literary style characteristic of a particular culture.

The Selected Bibliography at the end of the student text provides a wealth of resources for further reading and enjoyment.

2. *To Increase Awareness of Human Values, Attitudes, and Behavior.* The primary insight to be gained from the study of *World Mythology* is the fact that human beings are remarkably alike through time and across space. From the ancient Mesopotamians, Egyptians, and Greeks, living over three thousand years ago, to the peoples of Northern Europe, India, Japan, central Africa, and the Americas, and finally to those of us who live today, the needs and concerns of human beings have much in common. We still search for an explanation of how the universe was created and an explanation of the reasons behind changing seasons of the agricultural year. We still contemplate the nature of our fragile existence and concern ourselves with our own strengths and weaknesses. Each of us must still come to terms with our own mortality, the presence of evil in our lives, the extent to which we can determine the course of our own lives, and the extent to which the forces that limit our potential are beyond our control.

By introducing us to the values of many different cultures, *World Mythology* makes us aware of our own values and the extent to which we have acquired these values from particular cultures in the world. As we become aware of the underlying similarity among all cultures, we become more tolerant of others, recognizing that we are all members of the same human family.

We become accustomed to the idea that the great questions have more than one acceptable answer, and we learn to appreciate what we can learn from others whose ideas, values, and experiences may be quite different from our own.

3. *To Learn to Analyze Literature.* Mythology may be studied as the short story, drama, and novel are studied, with attention to specific kinds of literary analysis. Each myth should be considered in terms of the elements that exist in any work of fiction, including an appreciation of the function of:

   1. Plot—the chronological arrangement of events in the myth
   2. Setting—the time and place in which the events of the plot occur
   3. Characterization—the analysis of each of the major characters based upon:
      a. What the character thinks, says, and does
      b. What other characters think about, say, and do to this character
   4. Conflict—that which creates interest in the plot:
      a. One character or group of characters opposing another character or group of characters
      b. One character in conflict with him- or herself
      c. One character in conflict with society
      d. One character in conflict with the physical environment
   5. Crisis or turning point—the particular event that causes the plot to change direction
   6. Climax—the emotional high point of the plot (sometimes the same as the crisis)
   7. Theme—the underlying message or moral of the myth that is illustrated by the plot
   8. Irony—the opposite of what a character in the myth expects will happen
   9. Foreshadowing—hints in the form of seemingly inconsequential comments or events in the myth that pave the way for what will occur later in the plot
   10. Figures of speech, such as:
       a. Similes—the comparison of two different objects using *like* or *as* (example: as white as snow)
       b. Metaphors—the implied comparison of two different objects (example: snowy white)
       c. Homeric similes—similes recognized by their elaborate, lengthy comparison, originated by Homer but imitated by the authors of later epics
       d. Homeric epithets—particular descriptions of a character or an aspect of nature that function as appositives or as pronouns, originated by Homer but imitated by authors of later epics (examples: Hermes, the Wayfinder; Dawn, the rosy-fingered)
       e. Personification—attributing human characteristics to a nonhuman being, object, or concept (examples: Fate, Death)

f. Alliteration—choosing words that begin with the same sound in order to achieve a sense of pattern, unity, and a particular oral effect

In addition to providing exciting material for literary analysis, *World Mythology* provides excellent material for broadening students' vocabulary. The discussion of plot and the analysis of character should involve the study of words, both those actually used in a particular myth and other words that facilitate and enhance the discussion. For example:

1. Words that describe aspects of a character's personality
2. Words that describe aspects of the plot or setting
3. Greek and Latin prefixes and suffixes
4. Word derivations
5. Words derived from the names of mythological characters
6. Words that symbolize important concepts in a particular culture
   a. Greek: *aretē* (excellence in a particular area), *hubris* (excessive pride as a result of *aretē*), *atē* (rash or imprudent behavior as a result of *hubris*), and *nemesis* (retribution as a result of *atē*)
   b. Northern Europe and the British Isles: *wergild* (the payment of a specified amount of gold or treasure determined by the social status of a person who has been killed and in restitution for his or her death)
   c. India: *dharma* (righteous and proper behavior expected of each person depending upon his or her particular social position)
7. Cultural concepts
   a. Matriarchal society (a female-dominated, agricultural society in which people worship the Great Goddess or Mother Goddess as the primary divinity and the one who is responsible for the fertility of human beings, animals, and plants)
   b. Patriarchal society (a male-dominated society in which the principal divinity is male and the society is more aggressive and oriented toward progress)
   c. Chivalry (the code of behavior that knights in Northern European and British medieval literature take a sacred oath to obey)
   d. Reincarnation (rebirth in a new form of life: for example, a god reborn as a hero)
   e. *Yin* (in China, the dark, submissive, female principle in nature) and *yang* (the light, aggressive, male principle in nature)

USING WORLD MYTHOLOGY IN THE CLASSROOM

World Mythology is designed to facilitate a variety of teaching goals. One can read an individual myth as an independent work of literature, or read all of the myths from one part of the world, or compare the myths from one culture with those from a different culture, or study the myths by theme: creation, fertility, or hero. Consequently, you can devote anywhere from a day to a year to the study of *World Mythology,* depending upon how many myths are chosen and how much time is allowed for class discussion and creative projects.

The student's text opens with a general introduction that discusses the nature of myths, their common focus, and their purposes. These topics are followed by an explanation of matriarchal religion and a summary of major scholarly perspectives on mythology.

The myths themselves are then presented by culture in seven sections: The Middle East; Greece and Rome; The Far East and Pacific Islands; The British Isles; Northern Europe; Africa; and the Americas. Within each section the creation myth or myths are placed first, the fertility myth or myths second, and the hero myth or myths third. A cultural introduction opens each section, providing an overview of the myths that follow and introducing the reader to each of the myths found in that section.

A specific introduction precedes the presentation of each particular myth. This introduction prepares the reader by providing relevant historical background of the culture and the author, an explanation of the role of the gods and the heroic values in that culture, and a discussion of the appeal and value of the particular myth.

Extensive notes (provided at the end of the book) provide additional information about each myth, including other versions, sources, and additional reading.

The shorter myths can be discussed in a class session. The longer myths and epics have been divided into chapters ranging from approximately five to seven pages in length. These divisions lend themselves to a chapter-by-chapter discussion of the myth or epic, with at least one class period devoted to each chapter.

A Selected Bibliography of quality books, arranged by the sections into which *World Mythology* is divided, is provided at the end of the text for those who wish to do further reading. Both fine unabridged versions of the myths and background reading are included.

Also included in the student's text is an Index of Characters that will help students locate particular names. The Index also includes a pronunciation guide for most of the names listed.

Finally, the student text includes a list of provocative, open-ended questions for each myth. These questions appear at the end of the text. The questions are designed to encourage independent and creative thinking about characters and incidents, based upon close textual analysis of the facts and implications of events in the myth. You may choose to assign all or some of the questions for discussion, for written compositions, or for essay test questions. The nature and variety of the questions permits you to assign different questions to different classes.

COMPARATIVE MYTHOLOGY

World Mythology is designed to give you optimal teaching flexibility. Depending upon the time you wish to devote to the study of mythology and the particular subject matter of the course, you may choose to have students read one or more myths emphasizing a particular culture or emphasizing a comparison of particular cultures. For example, you can choose to study only creation myths or fertility myths or hero myths. You can choose to study only the most famous epics. Finally, you can choose to study the entire book, culture by culture, comparing one type of myth with others of the same type.

I have chosen the particular creation, fertility, and hero myths that are included from each culture because they reveal the values of the culture that produced them and because they relate to myths of the same type from other cultures. Certain myths form natural comparative units, but any two myths of the same type from different cultures provide an interesting comparison.

World Mythology is organized geographically by broad cultural area. The following table organizes the selections in *World Mythology* by type of myth.

SELECTIONS ORGANIZED BY TYPE OF MYTH

Creation Myths
The Enuma elish (Babylonia)
Osiris, Isis, and Horus (Egypt)
The Creation of the Titans and the Gods (Greece)
The Ages of Man (Greece)
Pyramus and Thisbe (Rome)
The Creation, Death, and Rebirth of the Universe (India)
The Creation of the Universe and Human Beings (China)
The Creation Cycle (New Zealand—Polynesia/Maori)
The Ages of the World (Ireland/Scotland—Celtic)
The Creation, Death, and Rebirth of the Universe (Northern Europe)
The Creation of the Universe and Ife (Nigeria—Yoruba)
The Origin of Life and Fire (Zaire—Boshongo/Bakuba)
The Creation (Bolivia—Tiahuanaco/Aymara)
Wanadi the Creator (Venezuela—Yekuhana)
The Creation (Guatemala—Maya)
The Creation Cycle (Mexico—Toltec/Aztec)
The Emergence (United States—Navajo)
The Woman Who Fell from the Sky (United States/Canada—Iroquois/Huron)
Sedna (United States/Canada—Inuit)

Fertility Myths
Telepinu (Hittite)
Demeter and Persephone (Greece)
Chi Li Slays the Serpent (China)
Amaterasu (Japan)
The Taming of the Sun (Polynesia/Hawaii)
Dagda the Good (Ireland/Scotland—Celtic)
The Death of Balder (Northern Europe)
The Quarrel Between Sagbata and Sogbo (Benin—Fon)
The Children of the Sun (Bolivia/Peru—Tiahuanaco/Aymara/Inca)

Wanadi, the Creator (Venezuela—Yekuhana)
Quetzalcoatl (Mexico—Toltec/Aztec)
The Woman Who Fell from the Sky (United States/Canada—
      Iroquois/Huron)
Raven and the Sources of Light (United States/Canada—
      Haida/Tsimshian/Tlingit)
Sedna (United States/Canada—Inuit)
Caught by a Hair-String (Canada—Micmac)

Hero Myths
The Traditional Hero
The Labors and Death of Heracles (Greece)
Chi Li Slays the Serpent (China)
The Taming of the Sun (Polynesia/Hawaii)
The Theft of Thor's Hammer (Northern Europe)
Lodge-Boy and Thrown-Away (United States—Crow)

The Culture Hero
Quetzalcoatl (Mexico—Toltec/Aztec)
Raven and the Sources of Light (United States/Canada—
      Haida/Tsimshian/Tlingit)
Caught by a Hair-String (Canada—Micmac)

The Epic Hero
Gilgamesh (Sumer/Babylonia)
Esfandyar (Persia)
The Iliad (Greece)
Jason and the Golden Fleece (Greece)
Medea (Greece)
The Aeneid (Rome)
The Ramayana (India)
Kotan Utunnai (Japan—Ainu)
Beowulf (England/Scandinavia)
King Arthur (England/France)
Sigurd the Volsung (Northern Europe)
Gassire's Lute (Faraka—Soninke)
Bakaridjan Kone (Segu)

TECHNIQUES FOR TEACHING SELECTIONS IN WORLD MYTHOLOGY

This section of the Manual includes suggestions for using the instructional aids that are included in *World Mythology*.

TEXT INTRODUCTION

Studies have shown that just as plants grow faster and stronger in fertile soil, students understand and remember what they read more easily, and therefore enjoy the process more, if they have received preparation for the reading assignment that will enable them to relate what they read to previously acquired background material and to similar myths.

Therefore, it is advisable to have students read the general introduction to *World Mythology* before reading any of the myths. The section titled "The Purpose of Myths" provides a strong foundation for the study of mythology in general and provides a general introduction to any one of the myths included in this book. The section titled "The Matriarchal Society" is important for the study of creation myths, particularly those of Greece and Babylonia.

SELECTION INTRODUCTIONS

It is imperative that students read the introduction to each myth before reading the myth itself. These introductions provide the historical background, the values of the particular culture, and the appeal and value of the myth that follows them.

If you plan to study more than one myth in a particular culture, it would be helpful to have students read the introduction to that particular section in order to receive an overview of the culture and of the myths in that section.

Always allow enough time to discuss the ideas presented in these sections and to answer any questions, for many of the ideas may be unfamiliar to your students.

READING AND DISCUSSING SELECTIONS

The reading of a myth or part of a myth can be either an in-class assignment or a homework assignment. Once the actual reading has been completed, be certain that everyone understands the factual content of the myth: what happened, to whom, and why. Refer back to the text to clarify any misunderstandings and ambiguities.

Have students read aloud their favorite part of a given myth and explain what they find most appealing about it. Share your own favorite passages with them also. Enjoyment is contagious, and the process of sharing increases the general enjoyment of the reading experience.

The shorter myths can be discussed in one or two class periods, depending upon the number of questions you choose to discuss, the number of students who participate, the extent of your own goals, and whether or not you compare one myth with a number of other myths.

The longer myths (the major epics) have been divided into chapters of approximately five to seven pages in order to facilitate discussion on a chapter-by-chapter basis. In general, allow one or two class periods per chapter, taking time to summarize the action of that particular chapter and to read selective passages aloud in order to clarify concepts, enjoy the conversations between particular characters, and appreciate literary style.

QUESTIONS FOR RESPONSE, DISCUSSION, AND ANALYSIS

Discussion and composition questions are listed by myth at the end of each myth, and suggestions for a range of answers to these questions follow in Part Two of this Manual. These questions are open-ended and interpretive, demanding that students use information stated or implied in a given myth to come to a variety of thoughtful conclusions.

The greater the variety of responses, the more interesting the discussion. However, each idea must have support within the myth. If necessary, have students read the part of the myth upon which they are basing their conclusions and discuss it.

In order to encourage students to volunteer opinions, accept all opinions that can be supported by facts and implications from the myth. Such an attitude on your part establishes an intellectual environment in which open inquiry, examination, and evaluation of the various aspects of a particular myth or group of myths can occur with ease. Only in such an accepting environment will any student who has an idea that can be documented gain the courage to express it.

Be careful not to praise "right" answers and criticize "wrong" answers, for in that environment, many students will not volunteer for fear of being wrong. Instead, question the student who volunteers. Ask him or her to explain the reasons for the opinion and to read aloud the parts of the myth in support of that particular point of view. Ask other students, one by one, whether they agree with the first student and to explain why or why not, again using passages from the myth itself to justify their opinions. In the course of this type of discussion, the student who is wrong will learn that he or she is wrong. Moreover, many other students may change or broaden their opinions as they hear ideas that did not originally occur to them.

Thus the students will learn from one another as well as from you, you will learn from them, and the entire class will acquire skill in making judgments based upon factual and implied information and in analyzing the opinions of others by evaluating the quality of their evidence. In this type of environment, intellectual inquiry is an exciting and challenging process. Those who experience it learn to be more analytical, critical, and flexible in their own thinking, more open to the ideas of others, and much more tolerant of people whose views differ from their own.

NOTES TO SELECTIONS

The Notes section at the back of the student text includes important information about the sources of each myth, as well as information about any abridgments or omissions. They include supplementary information about historical, religious, and literary background, as well as alternative versions. The Notes are especially useful if you and your students wish to do a more in-depth study of a particular myth or culture.

SELECTED BIBLIOGRAPHY

The Selected Bibliography at the end of the student text supplements the selections in *World Mythology*. This Bibliography includes additional sources for myths and information about the myths of various cultures, as well as a number of works that provide information about mythology as a subject for study. The works listed in the Bibliography can assist you in preparing your course and can provide students with valuable resources for further study.

INDEX OF CHARACTERS

The Index is designed to help you and your students locate characters within *World Mythology*. The Index is particularly helpful in revealing how various characters appear in different myths, sometimes across geographical and cultural lines. In order to facilitate classroom discussions and oral reading, pronunciations are provided wherever possible.

CREATIVE THINKING AND WRITING ACTIVITIES

Many of the questions in *World Mythology* lend themselves to expository compositions, which can be presented orally or in written form. These are good vehicles for teaching the writing skills necessary for formal, disciplined writing because the topics are stimulating and provocative, and the student is dealing with material that is enjoyable.

To supplement the text questions, the following list of creative thinking and writing activities emphasizes imaginative thinking and the creation of projects related to the myths in *World Mythology*. Offer your students a choice of activities based upon your own teaching goals, the needs and interests of your students, and the amount of time available for these activities.

Writing Activities
1. Write an original myth. For example:
   a. A creation myth that explains the origin of the universe or a particular country.
   b. A myth that explains some natural phenomenon.
   c. A myth describing the origin of any living thing or of any object.
   d. A destruction/re-creation myth that includes the cause, the punishment, and the rebirth.
   e. A fertility myth that involves either an insulted or deprived god or a god who rescues and restores.
   f. A myth that teaches a particular desirable behavior.
   g. A hero myth, set in either ancient or modern times.
2. Choose any myth in this book and write:
   a. A modern version: the characters, setting, and plot should be modern but the theme the same as in the original (e.g., Pyramus and Thisbe).
   b. A set of modern tasks or adventures for an ancient hero (e.g., Gilgamesh, Esfandyar, or Beowulf).
   c. A comic version or parody (e.g., Pyramus and Thisbe).
   d. An additional task or adventure set in ancient times (e.g., Esfandyar, Heracles, Aeneas, Sigurd, Beowulf).

    e. Supplementary material in the style of the original (e.g., the death of Achilles or a story about Maui).

    f. A different ending (e.g., to *The Iliad, Medea,* or *Beowulf*).

    g. A sequel (e.g., to *Jason and the Golden Fleece, Medea,* or "Caught by a Hair-String").

3. Retell one of the myths from the perspective of a different character. Choose any of the following suggestions or one of your own. Include the character's thoughts and feelings as well as his or her actions.

    a. Persephone describes her abduction by Hades and her captivity.

    b. Helen describes her abduction and her life in Troy during the war.

    c. Turnus describes the arrival of Aeneas and the ensuing war against the Trojans; Lavinia describes her engagement to Turnus and the events leading to her marriage to Aeneas; Aeneas' wife, Creusa, describes losing her husband and child as she tries to escape from Troy.

    d. Set describes his attempts to overthrow Osiris; Isis explains the treachery of Set and then her wish to save his life.

    e. Loki describes his part in the death of Balder and his own defeat.

    f. Grendel, his mother, or the dragon describes its encounter with Beowulf; a deserter describes Beowulf's last fight and his own desertion; Hrothgar's wife describes her life as queen and Grendel's threat to her safety.

    g. Guinevere describes her marriage to Arthur and her love of Lancelot; Mordred describes his feelings about Arthur and his treachery.

    h. Sita describes her captivity with Ravana and her later treatment by Rama.

    i. A citizen of Dierra describes Gassire's attitudes and behavior.

    j. Tezcatlipoca explains his feelings about Quetzalcoatl and describes his battle to overthrow him.

4. Write a play, radio script, or television script in which two or more heroes meet for the first time and discuss their attitudes, values, and experiences.

5. Pick your favorite hero from this book. Pretend that you are that hero as you do the following:

    a. Write a letter to a friend or relative explaining what you have learned from your adventures.

    b. Write an essay explaining an issue that concerns you, such as:

        (1) Why it is important to be a hero.

        (2) How a person becomes a hero.

        (3) Your attitude toward life and death.

6. Become an attorney. Prepare for a trial in which you must:

    a. Defend Sigurd against the charge of murdering Regin.

    b. Defend either Guinevere or Lancelot against charges of treason.

    c. Defend Sita against charges of infidelity.

    d. Defend Sedna's father against the charge of mutilating Sedna.

7. Prepare a debate in which Gassire and the hero you choose argue whether it is more important to be famous or more important to help one's family and community. Create arguments for both sides.

8. Become one of the gods or characters in these myths.
   a. Keep a journal of your thoughts and feelings as you experience the events in the myth, or write them to a friend or relative.
   b. Enter our century and visit the community where you live. Keep a diary of your activities and your reactions to modern life.
9. Prepare an interview with any god or character in this book, writing out both the questions and the answers. Make the character's answers reveal his or her personality and attitudes.
10. Write a character sketch.
   a. Show why the greatest hero is so great.
   b. Show why your favorite hero is your favorite.
11. A travel agent arranges for you to enter any part of one of these myths (e.g., the Underworld) on your vacation. Keep a daily journal of all that you see, your conversations, and your personal reactions.
12. You become a great hero. Write about your adventures as you would tell them to an interested listener.
13. Zeus or Vishnu grants you immortality. Write a letter to a friend or relative in heaven describing how you are using your endless life on earth.
14. Assume that the period in which we live follows the last period given in one of the creation myths. Describe our period.
15. Write a story about a person whose great skill leads to excessive pride, then to rash speech or action, and finally to punishment.
16. Write a story about a person whose greatest strength is also his or her greatest weakness.
17. Create a class newspaper or magazine where every article and advertisement is based on the myths in this book. Include news, sports, features, society, business, and advertisements.

Speaking Activities
1. With one or more of your classmates, dramatize any part of any myth in this book.
2. Using materials prepared by members of your class, conduct a debate to determine who is the world's greatest hero.
3. Read a myth that is not in this book and tell it to your class.
4. Read another version of one of the myths in this book—in the form of a play, novel, or poem—and tell that version to your class.
5. Show your class how artists have used one of these myths as the subject of a sculpture, painting, or drawing.
6. Show your class how musicians have used one of these myths as the subject of an opera, ballet, or orchestral composition.
7. Present a play or skit based on one of these myths.
8. Present a skit in pantomime and let your classmates guess your subject.
9. Become a talk-show interviewer. Choose a partner and interview one of the gods or other characters in one of these myths.
10. Become a god or character from one of these myths and play the game "Who Am I?" Give enough description so your classmates can guess who you are without making it either too easy or too difficult.

11. Read one of your creative compositions to your classmates.
12. Using arguments contributed by your classmates, conduct a debate between Gassire and another hero on the nature of heroism.

Art Activities
1. Make a diorama of a scene from one of the myths in this book.
2. Make a drawing, painting, or poster about one of these myths.
3. Create a sculpture of one of the famous monsters.
4. Make a collage of mythological allusions, themes, and places.
5. Make a scrapbook of mythological allusions in advertising, literature, and newspapers. Include a brief summary of the myth, providing the source of the allusion and showing why the allusion is used.
6. Take any product on the market today, and create a mythological allusion and advertising material for it.
7. Make charts comparing gods or heroes of different cultures.
8. Make diagrams of gods or heroes, showing family relationships.
9. Make a map of a hero's journey. Decorate it with the monsters he or she meets and other symbols of the hero's adventures.
10. Make a poster of articles on modern heroes.

EVALUATING STUDENTS' KNOWLEDGE AND SKILLS

The simplest tests test basic factual information, such as the identities of characters, which a student must know in order to understand and interpret a particular myth. The easiest test to create, to take, and to correct is the matching-type test. Multiple-choice, true-false, and fill-in-the-blank tests are equally easy to grade, but it is hard to create challenging tests of this type that reveal the knowledge of the student. They penalize the student who is a divergent thinker, the one who thinks of exceptions and sees ambiguities. Often, the teacher who creates a particular test of this type and then sets it aside for awhile will be uncertain of which answer is correct once he or she has forgotten the thinking that produced the question.

The short-answer and essay tests are much more indicative of a student's knowledge and ability to use higher-level thinking skills. They can measure comprehension, interpretation, and application of the concepts revealed in a particular myth or group of myths. The questions listed by myth at the back of the *World Mythology* text and discussed in this Manual are all of this type.

You may create additional questions of this type by having students use the myths they have read in *World Mythology* to

1. Analyze the nature of a particular character, god, or myth.
2. Analyze the behavior of a particular character or god.
3. Compare one character (or god, or myth) with another, giving both similarities and differences.
4. Read a new myth (at home or in class) from one of the cultures presented in *World Mythology*. Analyze it by discussing the type of myth it is and the

culture it represents based upon the nature of the characters, gods, events, and values it portrays.

5. Analyze a myth or group of myths that espouse a particular value or group of values, and explain how these myths transmit these values.

6. Analyze a different version of one of the myths in *World Mythology* and compare the two myths in terms of authenticity and style. Explain which is a better telling of the myth and why.

7. Analyze the role of the hero in a myth or group of myths.

8. Analyze the role of the gods in one or more of the epics.

9. Evaluate a value judgment, using a selection of myths to defend it or criticize it.

10. Read a myth (at home or in class) from a culture that is not included in *World Mythology* (example: Korean or Caribbean myths). Analyze the type of myth it is, the nature of the characters, gods, events, and values it portrays, and explain what it reveals about the culture that produced it.

11. Read a hero myth that is not included in *World Mythology* (example: Theseus, Meleager, or Perseus from Greek mythology). Analyze to what extent the principal character is a traditional hero. (Students should be able to recognize the following elements: (a) remarkable birth; (b) divine and royal parentage; (c) role of prophecy; (d) hero abandoned and reared in secrecy; (e) performs dangerous tasks; (f) visits the Underworld; (g) unhappy marriage; (h) error of judgment brings about violent death; (i) earns lasting fame.)

12. Read a particular modern short story or play (at home or in class) that has a mythological theme. Then discuss the mythological theme and explain how it enhances the meaning of the modern literary work.

Students must always be required to support their answers with evidence from the myth in the form of paraphrases of quotations, incidents, or examples. This approach motivates weak students to put forth greater effort, and it teaches good students to become more disciplined in their thinking.

Students also should be encouraged to outline their answers before beginning to write. This saves valuable time by forcing students to think through ideas before putting them in writing. It reveals false directions and weak points (those that cannot be easily or convincingly supported) before it is too late to redirect one's thinking, and it permits answers to be organized effectively. Having students outline their answers first and then turn in the outline with the essay question permits them to receive credit for knowledge that they did not have the time to write out.

Essay tests may be given as take-home assignments instead of given in class. The product is almost inevitably better because, without a time limit, a student is under much less pressure and can produce a better reasoned, better organized, and more detailed essay. However, the testing conditions cannot be monitored, and the result may be the product of collaboration instead of individual thinking.

Short-answer and essay-type questions are harder to grade than objective-type tests. It takes longer to read the answers, and you must formulate a grading scale that will be consistent by awarding the same number of points for the same type of answer. In this case, you may wish to write out the complete correct answer and assign a certain number of points for each part. With this in hand, you can then match each student's answer with the answer sheet. It is often easier and therefore faster to mark tests of this kind one question at a time, so that you can remember what the complete answer is and how many points you are assigning for each part.

PART 2

Teaching Selections in World Mythology

THE MIDDLE EAST

THE ENUMA ELISH (PAGE 3)

1. **Magical powers.** Marduk possessed the magic power to make a garment appear and disappear. Examples of other miraculous leaders include Zeus and Demeter, who can transform people into animals; Ishtar, who turns a shepherd who loves her into a wolf; Merlin, who can transform himself into anyone he chooses. Students may well know other famous incidents.

2. **Marduk versus Tiamat.** Marduk is superior to Tiamat in that all of the gods respect him and will obey him. Consequently, under his rule, order will prevail in the universe. He also organizes the universe so that the world becomes the one with which human beings are familiar.

3. **Creation of human beings.** The gods create human beings in order to have servants who will work for them. Consequently, their function is to serve the gods, a menial position. It follows from this that human beings would think little of themselves, viewing themselves as servants rather than as masters, and viewing the gods as having complete control over their lives. Human lives will revolve around activities designed to please gods.

OSIRIS, ISIS, AND HORUS (PAGE 12)

1. **Gods and life cycle.** The gods duplicate one another's general roles, possibly representing the fusion of a patriarchal religion with an earlier matriarchal religion. Isis and Osiris are both fertility gods, Isis being the Great Goddess or Mother Goddess and Osiris being her male counterpart. As such, Isis represents birth and Osiris may represent maturity.

   Like Demeter, Osiris teaches people how to raise crops and is the god of grain. When Osiris dies, Isis is able to bring him back to life temporarily, and later she is able to restore Horus to life when a scorpion has killed him. Finally, with the help of Horus, she and her sister restore Osiris to life permanently. In the end, Osiris represents death and resurrection, and Horus takes Osiris' place on earth as the god of grain. Isis remains the Great Goddess, one who is responsible for birth and rebirth.

2. **Set.** Set represents evil and the reality that evil is always a part of life. Therefore, Horus cannot kill him. Isis may free him to symbolize the eternal presence of evil in the universe. Students' opinions may vary as to whether the death of Set would have improved the myth.

TELEPINU (PAGE 22)

1. **Telepinu's behavior.** Telepinu behaves like a spoiled little boy who becomes very annoyed when something goes wrong, drops his toys, and goes off to his

room and sulks. Most students probably will not like him because he is so immature. It is hard to like someone who has such a volatile disposition and who wallows in self-pity.

2. **Mortals and Telepinu.** It was probably necessary for a mortal to pacify Telepinu because in real life mortals felt compelled to appeal to the god of fertility to help them. The role of the mortal in the myth symbolizes the role of mortals in actuality.

3. **Prayerlike chants at end of myth.** The chants are the way in which mortals convince Telepinu to return and help them. The myth contains so many ways of saying the same thing because the prayers are an emotional appeal. The repetition conveys seriousness, urgency, and intensity.

GILGAMESH (PAGE 26)

1. **Function of Enkidu.** Enkidu is created as a wild being in order to convey the idea that civilization is a positive aspect of life. Enkidu is brought from the darkness and ignorance of animal life into the light and knowledge of civilized life. Gilgamesh takes for granted and needs to learn to appreciate the material comforts and the psychological pleasures of the life he leads.

   In the process of becoming civilized, Enkidu loses his freedom to act just as he chooses. He must adopt codes of dress and behavior that make him acceptable to other human beings. Students' opinions may vary, but Socrates would say that it is better to be a man dissatisfied than a pig satisfied. Knowledge is better than ignorance, and it is worth the price.

2. **Gilgamesh as hero.** Gilgamesh has an immortal parent and the help of the gods, who give him the heroic qualities of great courage, strength, skill, and wisdom. However, in order to be immortal, a person must have two immortal parents. Gilgamesh performs a number of heroic feats: he is unsurpassed on the battlefield; he catches and kills the Bull of Heaven; he kills the monstrous giant Humbaba in the Cedar Forest of Lebanon; he travels to the end of the world, enduring hazards and deprivations in order to seek the advice of Utanapishtim.

   The gods are necessary in his life because their presence and aid provide an explanation for Gilgamesh's superiority (the implication being that if we had their help, we too could accomplish his deeds). However, they do not detract from Gilgamesh's heroism because they do not do very much for him. They cannot remove his fear or his sorrow, and they cannot grant him immortality. Psychologically, they leave Gilgamesh to cope with the stresses and strains of living, to accept the death of Enkidu, and to learn to accept his own mortality. Even his heroic feats are his and not theirs.

3. **Gilgamesh's journey.** Students' opinions may vary. It takes great courage to make a long, difficult, and dangerous journey into the unknown all alone. It takes courage to question rather than to accept blindly.

   Like many of the Greek heroes, Gilgamesh's stature is measured by the effort he makes to assert himself and change his fate. Gilgamesh loses the battle against his fate, as all mortals inevitably must, but the way he chooses to live his life establishes his greatness as a human being. He is a person to be admired and respected for his courage, his determination, and his perseverance. The fact that he becomes afraid makes him human; the fact that he acts courageously in spite of his fear makes him a hero.

4. **Gilgamesh and Enkidu.** Gilgamesh and Enkidu are almost twins. They are well matched in strength, intelligence, and courage. Each of them has moments of fear when the other bolsters his courage. Often, Enkidu looks ahead with fear, overcomes it, and then gives Gilgamesh advice as to how to proceed. At these times, he seems to function as Gilgamesh's inner self. Both have a very human fear of death. Enkidu dies because the gods choose to punish him and not Gilgamesh for killing the Bull of Heaven.

5. **Journey to Humbaba.** The author's emphasis upon the journey to find Humbaba rather than on the struggle reveals that courage is a particular mental outlook rather than a physical trait. Gilgamesh and Enkidu are heroes because they can conquer their fears. They have the strength and skill to kill Humbaba, but in order to be successful, they must have the courage to attempt it.

6. **Trials of Gilgamesh.** In order to be viewed as a hero, every person must withstand trials and accomplish difficult feats. Gilgamesh must learn to live as a wild man in order to reach Utanapishtim. He must kill animals and wear their skins for warmth and protection. He must forage for wild plants and kill wild animals for feed. He must defend himself against predators. He must be courageous, determined, resourceful, and skillful if he is to survive the journey. Moreover, he must be able to cope with every stress and danger alone. The greater the trials, the greater the hero who surmounts them.

7. **Utanapishtim's message.** Gilgamesh learns that no plan exists whereby a mortal can become immortal. Utanapishtim was chosen by the gods to have everlasting life; he did nothing to deserve it, nor did he set out to achieve it. It was conferred upon him by divine decree. Utanapishtim proceeds to list for Gilgamesh the many gifts he has received from the gods, gifts that make him the most fortunate and superior of human beings. Gilgamesh accepts his destiny because he has no choice. He cannot even pass Utanapishtim's test of strength.

8. **How knowledge changes Gilgamesh.** The knowledge Gilgamesh acquires changes his life in that he learns to appreciate his blessings. He has the joy of life, family, kingship, and the everlasting fame of heroic deeds. He has the opportunity to teach his people to become wise about their own lives. He has the wealth and power to build monuments that will last long after he has died and will testify to his greatness. Consequently, Gilgamesh builds monuments and instructs his people, gaining immortality in the only ways possible for human beings.

9. **Character of Gilgamesh.** Students' answers may vary. Possible answers include: courageous: fights Humbaba and the Bull of Heaven; takes a long,

arduous journey in search of immortality; determined: continues his journey despite the hardships of lack of food and clothing, danger of wild animals, and discouragement from everyone he meets along the way; ambitious: wants to achieve fame so that people will always remember him and immortality so that he will live forever; caring: dear friend of Enkidu (adjectives of this nature are less appropriate, because Gilgamesh's search is not to help Enkidu, but to help himself: Gilgamesh wants to prevent his own death).

10. **Journey for knowledge.** Students' answers may vary. Today a person may make a dangerous journey in order to acquire knowledge by traveling into outer space.

Supplementary Questions

1. Do you like Gilgamesh? Why or why not?

2. What do you think makes life worth living?

3. Many heroes experience a symbolic form of death that separates their old life from a new life in which they see more clearly and understand more completely. In literature, this spiritual journey can occur in a dream or in an actual adventure, and it is called a "night journey."

   Consider one of the following heroes from the myths or epics that you have read. What effect does the hero's experience in or with the Underworld have upon his life: (a) Heracles? (b) Aeneas? (c) Gilgamesh?

ESFANDYAR, THE PRINCE WHO WOULD BE KING (PAGE 58)

1. **"The Seven Stages."** Esfandyar probably is a hero from a heroic tradition that competed with the heroic tradition of Rostam from Seistan. In such instances, the later hero gains stature by imitating the heroic exploits of the earlier hero. Consequently, it is important to Esfandyar's audience that he can do what Rostam did. A similar relationship exists between Heracles (Hercules) of Argos and Theseus of Athens, who is a later Greek hero.

2. **Simurgh's advice and Rostam's behavior.** Because Esfandyar is the prophet of Zardosht and also the son of the king who is in line to inherit the rule of Persia, Ferdowsi probably intends readers of the *Shahnameh* to interpret the simurgh's advice to mean that Rostam should go in chains to King Goshtasp. It is the mark of Rostam's pride that he consistently refuses to do this, even accepting his own dire prophecy. When Rostam says that he has nothing to lose, he may well be correct, because it is another issue whether (later) Shaghad would have killed him even without this unrelated incident.

3. **Responsibility for Esfandyar's death.** (a) Esfandyar is responsible for his own death because his desire for his father's throne and his religious principles are more important than anything else. However, although Esfandyar

always cites his religious principles in defense of his actions, after Rostam mortally wounds him, he blames his father for his death and says that his father's actions have incurred the enmity of Zardosht. (b) Rostam is responsible for Esfandyar's death because his pride makes it impossible for him to follow the simurgh's advice, despite the fact that he knows that the Bird of Marvel knows what is best for him. (c) Goshtasp is responsible for Esfandyar's death because he puts his son in the position where he cannot refuse his father's command. To do so would defy parental and regal authority and the religious principles by which he lives. (d) The simurgh is responsible in that it tells Rostam the only way that it is possible to kill Esfandyar. Consequently, all four appear to have an equal share in the responsibility. If any one had responded differently, the tragedy would not have occurred.

4. **Goshtasp and Esfandyar.** Both Goshtasp and Esfandyar are responsible for the disastrous nature of their relationship. Goshtasp is more to blame than Esfandyar in that he distrusts his son and believes whatever evil tales ambitious nobles relate about him. Goshtasp is certain that Esfandyar's ambition to be king of Persia will lead him to take his father's crown and throne, just as Goshtasp took the crown and throne of Persia from his own father. Goshtasp is so vulnerable on this point that he believes that Esfandyar would even kill him in order to do it, although he did not kill his own father.

Although Goshtasp is a convert to Zoroastrianism, his fear of his son's behavior is stronger than his belief in his new religion. Therefore, their mutual ambitions to be king of Persia prevent Goshtasp from thinking good thoughts, speaking good words, and performing good deeds in connection with Esfandyar, and they prevent him from understanding how devout a believer Esfandyar is and, therefore, how little a threat he is to his father's power.

Esfandyar is a prophet of Zardosht, and he lives according to Zoroastrian moral principles. Although he wishes to become king of Persia, he wants to earn the title through his heroic deeds, and he wants his father to give him his kingdom as a reward. Esfandyar has no intention of usurping his father's power, and, consequently, his father's fears about him are unfounded since they do not recognize Esfandyar's religious principles.

Esfandyar's issues are complex. He must decide what the true Zoroastrian does when his father and king commands him to do something that is both clearly unjust and unnecessary. His choice is either to refuse to bring Rostam to Goshtasp, even though his refusal to obey his father and king would violate the religious principles by which he lives, or to confront Rostam and accept whatever consequences follow from this deed, thereby obeying his father and king and adhering to his religious principles.

Esfandyar never understands, nor seeks to understand, the factors that lead his father to fear his ambition. Therefore, he never addresses these issues. He simply sees his father as a manipulator and a man who refuses to keep his word, both of which he is. However, given that Goshtasp had longed to possess his father's crown and throne, it is not likely that Esfandyar could have convinced Goshtasp to change his opinion of him.

Esfandyar lives his life according to the principles of Zoroastrianism in that he always obeys the commands of his father and king. His great deeds and his adherence to his religious principles make him a great hero to those who agree with his values. His ambition makes him very human.

5. **Esfandyar as tragic hero.** Esfandyar's ambition causes his tragedy in that it alienates his father, who indirectly causes his death. His ambition also prevents him from compromising in any way in order to make peace with Rostam and thus save his own life. Esfandyar's religious piety also causes his tragedy in that it prevents him from disobeying the command of his father and king.

Esfandyar is a tragic figure in that he recognizes the role of ambition in his life in his unrelenting determination to win the crown and throne of Persia from his father. He also realizes that, given the obedience that he owes his father and king, and the role of religion in his life, he must prepare to die for the values by which he lives. However, although Esfandyar understands the extent to which he is the cause of his own situation, he blames his father, rather than himself, for his death.

6. **Fate and prophecy.** Prophecies are a manifestation of Fate. They reveal what is going to happen but without revealing how it will occur. In works of literature, they therefore create a particular type of interest or suspense for the reader.

It is interesting that, in cultures where prophecies are important, the literary characters may or may not make an attempt to avoid them. In this legend, Goshtasp acts upon the prophecy about Esfandyar's death in order to hasten it. However, the nature of prophecy assumes that Goshtasp will behave as he does. Goshtasp is able to manipulate Esfandyar because he can make Esfandyar's ambition and religious principles work against Esfandyar's own best interests. Despite Esfandyar's conflict with his father, he becomes a great hero who dies for what he wants and believes.

Since such prophecies always come to be, they reinforce the idea that human beings are constructed so as to bring about their own fate. Fate has determined the end, and each person's human nature, given its limitations, will accomplish the rest. Therefore, prophecies darken the tone of a literary work because they reveal that human beings have little control over their actions and the course of their lives. As these prophecies become fulfilled, they call attention to the nature of the human condition, with its inescapable mortality, its many tragedies, the limited ability to control the course of one's life, and the transitory nature of all the good things in life.

7. **Simurgh's contribution.** The simurgh contributes the quality of magic to the legend. The Bird of Marvel's role is to save Dastan and his family from disaster. The blood from another simurgh makes Esfandyar invulnerable to injury.

The simurgh is also an instrument of Fate. By preserving Zal's life, it assures Rostam's birth. By making Esfandyar invulnerable to injury, it preserves his life and enables him to become a great hero. By telling Rostam how to kill Esfandyar, it assures Esfandyar's death and gives Rostam the burden of having killed a prince who was in line for the throne of Persia. The simurgh tells Rostam that this offense will determine the nature of his own death.

8. **Predetermination and life-experience.** Those who believe in a controlling Fate can go through life with a freedom that others may not feel because they know that they cannot control the timing of their death. Consequently, they may feel more comfortable taking risks since these will not cause them to die before their time. However they and others choose to act, they feel that it was predetermined that they would act as they have chosen to do.

   Those who do not believe in a controlling Fate believe that a person possesses the ability to have a role in determining his or her own fate. These people may make more of an effort to improve their lives and to help the society in which they live, on the theory that how they choose to live their lives can make a difference to themselves and to others.

9. **Use and contribution of repetition.** Particular words and phrases are used repeatedly in connection with people, the passage of time, and scenes of war. For example, the epithet *Rostam the Mighty* repeatedly describes Rostam; particular descriptions of the sun describe particular times of day; and a set paragraph repeatedly describes the bloody battlefield when Persian warriors confront the Turanians in battle. These repetitive devices unify the myth and enhance its effect by making it possible for readers to visualize Rostam and certain scenes in the myth.

GREECE AND ROME

THE CREATION OF THE TITANS AND THE GODS (PAGE 82)

1. **Gaea as human mother.** The Greek gods are anthropomorphic in that they think, feel, act, and speak the way that human beings do. The Greeks looked at their own existence and created a divine family that mirrored the families that they saw around them, both in terms of personality and in terms of power structure. Like the human family, the divine family consists of successive generations of children, with each generation jealous of the power of their elders and anxious to capture it for themselves.

   Gaea is like a human mother in that she is a loving, devoted, protective mother. When Uranus imprisons her monstrous children deep within her, she hates him enough to encourage her most courageous son to remove his father from power with the hope that he will also rescue his monstrous brothers. The fact that Gaea plays such a powerful role in the creation myth reflects the earlier matriarchal culture that was dominated by females.

2. **Zeus better than Uranus and Cronus.** Zeus is a better leader than either Uranus and Cronus because the Greeks who created this myth believed that the world was progressing from chaos to order. Such an optimistic view of the world reflects the feeling that they were gaining control over their environment. They still needed the help of the gods if they were to survive, but they possessed greater technology than their ancestors. Agriculture permitted them to live in stable communities where, weather permitting, the tended fields would yield crops season after season. Consequently, Zeus is not only more intelligent than Cronus, he is less monstrous. When Cronus swallows his first five children, he is a savage. When Zeus swallows his wife Metis, so that she will not give birth to a child who will destroy him, he is clever.

3. **Combining patriarchal and matriarchal religions.** The reign of Zeus represents the conquest of the matriarchal societies in Greece by the invading patriarchal societies. The roles of Gaea and Rhea in Greek mythology reveal that female gods continue to wield some power and command great respect. Both Gaea and Rhea are opinionated, courageous, and clever. Faced with adversity, both wait for a propitious occasion and then take vengeance upon their respective husbands. Zeus's first wife will be Metis, the wisest of the Titan goddesses. When he swallows her, she continues to give him advice, and he too becomes very wise.

THE AGES OF MAN (PAGE 90)

1. **The best age.** So many changes occur in a person's lifetime that it is not unusual for an older person to think that things are not as good as they used to be. People often long for "the good old days" when everything was familiar and predictable. Looking back to the time of youth, adults often see this

period as a carefree time of all play and no work, forgetting the anxieties that accompany youth. Consequently, the first age is the best, and the ages become progressively worse as they approach the time in which Hesiod, the author of this myth, is living.

However, more than "rose-colored glasses" may be involved. Hesiod may have known of agricultural communities that existed long before his time that were peaceful, passive, and generous. In these communities, progress was not a value: everyone lived like everyone else, having no more and no less and sharing whatever one had with neighbors. Because the earth was worshipped as the Great Goddess or Mother Goddess, people felt an obligation to care for the land and water and to leave it to their children in the condition they had received it from their parents. They took no more than they needed, and they wasted little of what they took.

2. **Age of Iron and modern times.** It is so customary for people to think that they are living in the worst age in history that periodically newspapers publish essays written in earlier periods that read as if they could have been written today. Like the people living in Hesiod's age, we too have lives filled with work and grief. We too face death. Many of us have lived through the greatest crimes one group of human beings has ever perpetrated against another group, and we can give more than one example of inhumane behavior. One can cite the violence that occurs in our cities and the fact that many people make the acquisition of wealth their principal objective. We take everything in nature that we find useful, leaving us with environmental problems, such as erosion and pollution. Many of us have lived through a number of wars. Many feel that their children ignore them once they become old, weak, and dependent. Consequently, this passage in Hesiod is one of the most powerful in all of mythology.

3. **Human nature.** It is more accurate to draw conclusions about human beings who live in societies that share certain common values than it is to make blanket statements about all human beings. Our society has many values in common with the society in which Hesiod lived, most notably the concept of progress. Peoples who are interested in improving their lives traditionally have been more aggressive and acquisitive. They have been warrior societies, and they have valued material possessions and wealth. This is one of the major distinctions between the patriarchal society (Hesiod's and ours) and the matriarchal society.

DEMETER AND PERSEPHONE (PAGE 93)

1. **Zeus's personality and power.** In this myth, Zeus is presented as the most powerful of the Olympian gods. Both Hades and Demeter turn to him for help, and both obey him. Zeus is intelligent and reasonable; he understands both Hades' and Demeter's points of view; and he solves problems by means of compromise. The universe operates under the direction of Zeus; it is he who establishes and maintains order, both among the Olympian gods and among human beings.

2. **Greek gods as anthropomorphic.** Hades is very human in that, despite his great power, he dislikes his dark, dismal kingdom. It is not surprising that he would love Persephone and want to bring the sunshine and laughter she radiates into his land. Although he is dreaded and feared, he can be loving and kind.

   Demeter is one of the greatest mothers in literature. One cannot escape the power of her anguish as she searches the world for her kidnapped daughter. Every reader feels her deep love for her daughter and her anger, hatred, and horror at Persephone's abduction. We can understand her vengeance even if we do not condone it.

   Rhea too is a loving mother, who understands her daughter's anguish and tries to persuade her to accept compromise in life.

   Persephone has a minor role, but she is human as she is torn between the husband and the mother who both love her.

   Zeus, as the beneficent father-king, tries his best to keep everyone satisfied.

3. **Cyclical nature of life.** Demeter represents motherhood, maturity, and a rich agricultural harvest. Hades represents death, the earth from which new life emerges each spring. Persephone represents birth, youth, and rebirth. She is the eternal spring, annually giving birth to new plant life and bringing the hope of survival and prosperity to human beings.

THE LABORS AND DEATH OF HERACLES (PAGE 100)

1. **Heroic qualities.** Heracles is the most famous Greek hero because of his personality and because of the deeds he performs for society. He is courageous, strong, skillful, persevering, sorry for his mistakes, loyal to his friends, unrelenting toward his enemies, and wants to make the world a safer place. Interestingly enough, unlike many other heroes, the idea of immortality does not impress him. He knows that he will attain it, but he performs the deeds he does for the personal challenge and sense of accomplishment and for the good of other people.

2. **Visit to the Underworld.** The visit to the Underworld is one of the characteristics of the hero myth. It represents the ultimate in mustering courage and facing death. Most heroes learn something of importance in the Underworld that changes the course of their lives. At the least, the hero learns to value life and achievements on earth.

3. **Strengths.** Students' answers will vary. Many will credit their parents; others will credit their friends. This works well as a writing assignment. If written, students should give examples of the ways in which the people they have chosen actually help them.

4. **Performing dangerous labor.** Students' answers will vary. Some will say fame; other responses might be power, glory, wealth, love, self-respect, or survival.

1. Does the fact that Heracles becomes immortal make him a greater hero? Why or why not?

2. Which of Heracles' labors is your favorite? Why?

THE ILIAD (PAGE 106)

1. **Responsibility to self and community.** Students' answers will vary. As leaders, the five men must place the welfare of the soldiers under their command before the needs of their families and themselves. Since the Greeks received self-esteem from what others thought of them, if they lived in such a way that they gained the approval of others, they received what they wanted for themselves: public honor. (a) Agamemnon has the obligation of uniting the Greeks under his leadership. If he cannot do this, the Greeks will disintegrate into a number of jealous, warring factions, which, in fact, was usually the case among the ancient Greeks. He must treat the other leaders in such a way that they will respect his leadership and will obey him. He must show that he respects them. (b) Achilles is caught between his need for public honor and the duty that he owes to Agamemnon. He owes Agamemnon obedience, yet he is owed public respect. The Greeks support him when he withdraws from the war. Only when he refuses to accept Agamemnon's apology and gifts do the Greeks think that he is at fault. (c) Patroclus is obligated to obey Achilles. He achieves more than enough honor to the extent that he does what Achilles asked him to do, which is to rout the Trojans from the Greek ships. (d) Hector, as commander of the Trojans and their allies, must put the welfare of his city before the needs of his family and his personal desires. He owes it to himself to behave in a way that makes him and his family proud, and, like the Greeks, he achieves this by acting in such a way so as to gain public approval. (e) Paris owes as much as Hector to the Trojans, because his actions caused the war. He owes it to himself to act in such way that he has self-esteem. The problem seems to be that Paris is content to set his own standards for his behavior. He is satisfied to judge himself, and what others think of him and say about him does not bother him. He is good-natured and well-meaning, but present pleasure means more to him than earning honor and glory on the battlefield.

2. **Quarrel between Achilles and Agamemnon.** Homer chooses a more interesting topic than the glorification of heroic exploits. He focuses on the behavior of warriors in time of crisis, because it is under stress that people reveal their basic natures. Achilles' quarrel with Agamemnon examines the way that an individual leader's view of himself affects his behavior and his values. Agamemnon's arrogant treatment of Achilles comes close to causing the Greeks to lose the war. Achilles' refusal to accept Agamemnon's apology causes the death of his best friend, a risk that never occurred to Achilles because he was too preoccupied with his own reputation to think of Patroclus.

3. **Reputation versus wealth and power.** Students' answers may vary. Certainly a person's reputation lives on long after he or she has died, and in the Greek culture as in our own, people did not believe that they could use their wealth and power after they died.

4. **Argument over a woman.** Homer chooses an argument over a woman as the cause of the tragic quarrel because Briseis, as a prize of honor, is the greatest of all prizes for the greatest Greek fighter. However, it does not matter what causes the quarrel. What is important to Homer are the widespread consequences of the argument, and he spends the entire epic following the ramifications of the disagreement.

5. **Character of Agamemnon.** Agamemnon is an arrogant, unimaginative person who cannot handle the position of leadership that his wealth and political power have thrust upon him. It is more important to him that he have a prize of honor that is, in fact, simply a badge of his position than it is to keep his best fighter on the battlefield. He is so vain that he is overly sensitive to the possibility of slights to his honor, and he ignores the advice of Nestor, the wisest elder statesman of the Greeks. Agamemnon is so insecure and vain that he will not part with his badge unless another great man, Achilles, parts with his badge. Agamemnon is promised even greater prizes in the future, but, like a child, he insists upon immediate gratification.

   Agamemnon fails the leadership test because he causes his greatest fighter to withdraw. He fails the personality test because he is arrogant, vain, selfish, and insensitive to the feelings and needs of anyone except himself. His only success comes when he apologizes to Achilles and offers him any number of gifts. Yet, Achilles is right in believing that Agamemnon has not really changed. Although Odysseus wisely does not repeat to Achilles the end of Agamemnon's speech, Agamemnon still wants Achilles to realize that he, Agamemnon, is the greater and more powerful man. Also, Agamemnon sends emissaries to go to Achilles. He does not go himself, because he views that as demeaning.

   Moreover, Agamemnon is a coward. Whenever the Greeks are in grave trouble, he suggests returning to Greece, much to the chagrin of Odysseus. Consequently, in spite of whatever deeds he performs on the battlefield, Agamemnon does not appear to be a hero at all.

6. **Agamemnon through Achilles' eyes.** Achilles sees Agamemnon quite accurately. (a) Agamemnon apologizes to Achilles only because the Greeks are in such dire straits that he will lose command if he does not. (b) He gives Achilles a superabundance of gifts so that his offer will place Achilles in the wrong if he rejects it. He cannot afford to have anyone say that Achilles refused his offer because he did not offer enough wealth. (c) Agamemnon follows Nestor's suggestion in sending Ajax and Odysseus to Achilles. An advantage is that they are Achilles' closest friends, next to Patroclus. However, Achilles might have been more receptive had Agamemnon chosen to make his offer personally.

7. **Character of Achilles.** Like Agamemnon's, Achilles' behavior is juvenile. When he is publicly insulted, he wants all of the Greeks to be punished so that they will miss his participation in the war. This is the ultimate in self-centered behavior. Achilles is as arrogant as Agamemnon in that, as the greatest Greek fighter, he will not take second place to his commander-in-chief. He feels that the greatest honor is earned on the battlefield by a warrior, and that other skills, such as leadership and strategy, come second. When Achilles sends Patroclus into the war, he directs him to win honor for Achilles but to refrain from winning honor for himself because that will diminish Achilles' honor.

Achilles has very little self-control: he cannot resist the temptation to wallow in self-pity at the cost of a multitude of deaths; he cannot control his pride and vanity; and he cannot control his anger and vindictiveness. Only with Priam does Achilles manage any self-control at all, but he warns Priam how close to losing it he is. When Achilles kills Hector, his treatment of Hector's body is despicable.

Homer shows that the line between man and beast is very thin—socialization is but a veneer. The qualities that make a warrior victorious on the battlefield are not the qualities that make him a decent human being. Consequently, given the aspect of Achilles that Homer presents, Achilles' heroic image is clouded by his vanity, his self-centeredness, his emotionality, and his beastliness.

8. **Why Achilles withdraws from battle.** This is a question that elicits a number of responses. He does love Briseis, but that is not the reason. In Greek society, self-esteem is determined by public recognition of one's worth, and Briseis represented the public recognition of Achilles' worth. Consequently, to be deprived of her is an insult to his honor, and his pride will not permit him to tolerate such a public insult to his honor.

9. **Achilles' options.** (a) When Achilles remains by his ships, he could choose to return home, but his father would criticize his behavior as embarrassingly juvenile. (b) He has to let Agamemnon take Briseis, because he would win no honor by killing his commander. However, to let him do so without protest would be demeaning. Achilles is entitled to protest, and the Greeks accept that. (c) He should accept Agamemnon's gifts, because they are a fitting tribute to his social status and to his worth as a warrior. However, he feels that accepting the gifts would make him subservient to Agamemnon. In fact, Achilles is subservient, but he is too proud and arrogant to acknowledge that. (d) Achilles should not send Patroclus into battle. He should go himself. Patroclus is a fine warrior, but not the warrior that Achilles is. Obviously, he cannot succeed as well as Achilles can, and anyone but Achilles would realize the risk that Patroclus was taking. At this point, Achilles should accept Agamemnon's gifts and apology, late as it is, arguing that their disagreement was causing great harm to the Greek forces and that he intended to save them from the Trojans. Such a statement would win him the public acclaim that means so much to him. (e) Although Achilles has lost all sense of perspective,

he is not so self-centered that he will keep both himself and Patroclus out of battle. He still has some sense of public duty. To see the Greeks devastated tears at his heart, and he feels enough guilt to let Patroclus fight in his place. Besides, to keep both of them out of battle under these circumstances would damage his reputation beyond repair.

10. **Achilles' criticism of warrior society.** It is likely that Achilles questions the values by which his society operates because he has become Agamemnon's victim. He is the best Hellenic warrior, and yet his commander is depriving him of his reward (his prize of honor, Briseis) and the public esteem that accompanies this reward. Achilles is most unusual in his ability to remove himself from a situation and analyze it (as he also does with Priam on the nature of blessings and sorrows in one's life). However, student opinion will vary as to whether Achilles is so unusual that he would have been motivated to question the nature of his society's rewards as long as he was receiving all that he had earned.

Achilles objects to the fact that he takes greater personal risks and accomplishes more in battle than Agamemnon does, because he fights at the front of the Greek forces while Agamemnon either brings up the rear or remains with his ships. Yet, because Agamemnon is the commander-in-chief of the Greeks, Agamemnon views it as his right to choose the best and the greatest number of prizes from whatever the other Greeks, including Achilles, bring from the cities they have raided. Achilles also objects to the fact that the other Greek leaders condone Agamemnon's attitudes and behavior.

Students' opinions may vary as to the extent to which Achilles' objections are valid. Some may think that Agamemnon is entitled to take fewer risks and greater personal enrichment because his position entitles him to these benefits. Others may think that the spoils of battle should be distributed strictly according to each warrior's merit on the battlefield, regardless of rank.

The fact that the other Greek leaders condone Agamemnon's attitudes is typical of human behavior. As long as each man is satisfied with his own rewards, he is not likely to push for a change in the system of distribution since, under new rules, he might not prosper as well. The other Greek leaders are interested in supporting whatever actions will bring the Greek war against Troy to a quick and successful conclusion, so that they can return home. Therefore, it is in their own best interest for Achilles to agree to reenter the war. Ajax and Odysseus pressure Achilles to accept Agamemnon's gifts for their own benefit, rather than for the benefit of Agamemnon or Achilles.

11. **Achilles as tragic hero.** (a) Achilles is a tragic figure because he must sacrifice his life in order to achieve the immortality conferred by lasting fame. His choice between a long life without fame or a short life with eternal fame is tragic because, in the end, he does not really have that choice to make. Once Patroclus has been killed, Achilles is obligated to avenge his death, thus bringing on his own death as well. (b) Achilles leaves the war in order to teach Agamemnon how important it is to value the leaders under his

command and also to teach the other Greek leaders that it was actually in their own best interest to have supported Achilles in the argument. Therefore, it is tragic that Achilles must reenter the war before his action has accomplished his goals. Achilles knowingly chooses to die, not for the Greek cause, nor in order to preserve his own honor as a hero, but in order to preserve his personal honor as Patroclus's friend. He sees the irony of his situation. Having insight into his own needs, interests, and values, as well as those of Agamemnon and the other Greek leaders, he reveals a profound understanding and acceptance of the human condition. (c) The other Greek leaders may be courageous and skillful on the battlefield, but they seem to be unable or unwilling to understand Achilles' point of view. Even Ajax and Odysseus, Achilles' closest friends among the Greek leaders, speak from self-interest and self-pity and therefore willingly serve as Agamemnon's agents when they attempt to persuade Achilles to reenter the war. (d) It is tragic that Achilles so needs to be honored by his peers that he leaves the battle to the others, hoping that his absence will be sorely felt, while at the same time those whose honor he seeks do not understand or value what he himself values. Students may wish to discuss what value the honor acquired under such conditions would have for Achilles.

12. **Achilles' immortality.** If Homer had included the notion of Achilles' immortality, his audience likely would have accepted it as being the just reward for a great Greek hero and also as being consistent with the fate of heroes in other Greek myths. For example, Heracles' heroic feats cause Zeus to make Heracles immortal.

Students will probably differ as to how Achilles' immortality would affect their own response to *The Iliad*. Death gives a validity and an intensity to the decisions we make during the course of our lives. When we believe we cannot live forever, each moment has greater value, and our decisions are important. The certainty of Achilles' death makes each of his decisions a serious matter, with far-ranging, irreversible, and tragic consequences. In contrast, Achilles' immortality, if he knew about it, would turn his life into a game; while if he did not know about it, his immortality would remove the tragedy and—even more important—the human condition that Achilles shares with others.

13. **Responsibility for Patroclus's death.** As is characteristic of Greek myth, Patroclus's responses to the particular situations that he confronts make him most responsible for his own fate. Other characters have limited responsibility: (a) Nestor suggests that Patroclus wear Achilles' armor, lead the Myrmidons in battle against the Trojans, and push them back from the Greek ships. (b) Achilles does not choose to fight for himself but instead agrees to let Patroclus fight in his place. (c) Patroclus disobeys Achilles' strict orders to return to the Greek ships once he has pushed the Trojans a safe distance back toward Troy. Patroclus so enjoys his victories that he continues to push on toward Troy until he reaches the great wall, where he persists even against Apollo. He is fighting to achieve heroism for himself, rather than for

the benefit of the Greeks or Achilles, and he is responsible for the consequences. (d) Apollo enhances Patroclus's reputation as a hero by being the first to stop him. Patroclus is such a great warrior that unless Apollo intervened, even Hector would have had a difficult time defeating him. (e) The Trojan who first wounds Patroclus in the back enables Hector to approach and kill Patroclus. By being one of the three warriors necessary to kill Patroclus, he also enhances Patroclus's reputation as a hero. (f) Hector is responsible for Patroclus's death simply because he is its final cause. This enhances Patroclus's reputation because it takes three warriors to kill him, but it diminishes Hector's reputation on the battlefield because he was not the sole cause of Patroclus's death.

14. **Why Apollo weakens Patroclus.** Homer has Apollo weaken Patroclus before others kill him as a way of demonstrating how great a warrior Patroclus is. The implication is that if Apollo had not weakened Patroclus, no one would have been able to kill him.

15. **Hector.** Hector is a very appealing person. On the surface, Hector is the opposite of Achilles in that he always puts the needs of his people before the wishes of his family, whereas Achilles puts himself first and the Greeks second.

    However, Hector is also very much like Achilles, because his pride is as great as Achilles'. Hector thinks only of what others will say about him. In order to win their approval, he puts them first. He is so anxious to prove his courage and skill that he ignores the excellent advice of Polydamas and stays on the battlefield once Achilles reenters the fight, even though it would have been far wiser to have fought from the Trojan wall. Hector's pride will not let him make the intelligent choice, and consequently Hector is responsible for causing the deaths of many of his warriors, as well as his own death. Yet Hector remains an appealing hero. We do not expect heroes to be perfect, and we can understand and identify with Hector's weaknesses.

16. **Hector's fear of Achilles.** Hector's fear enhances Achilles and Hector. It strengthens Achilles' skills as a warrior to have such a great warrior as Hector afraid of him. It strengthens Hector's courage when he accepts the fact that he will die and fights Achilles anyway, because that is courage mustered in the face of terror. Many students will feel that when Hector runs from Achilles, he is a coward. However, to run from certain death may be sensible, and certainly it is what many human beings would do. Psychologically, it gives Hector time to accept the fact that he is going to have to stop and face the inevitable.

17. **Athena's deception of Hector.** This part of *The Iliad* may cause readers great trouble. Athena is one of the most appealing of the Greek divinities, and many readers will find it despicable that she tricks Hector. Moreover, there appears to be no other way to explain the circumstance. Usually, we attribute the roles of the Greek gods to other causes, but it is hard to see how Deiphobus could have disappeared without Hector's being aware of it. Many readers feel that this episode would have been more effective if it had

involved an event or a character's motivation that we could understand. However, unlike the breaking of Paris's helmet-strap, Deiphobus's disappearance cannot be explained as chance.

18. **Hector's choices.** Once Hector knows that Troy is doomed to lose the war, he has no viable choice except to continue fighting. If he quits, he is a coward. He must continue to be an inspiration to his people. The person who retreats when the going gets tough is viewed as Odysseus views Agamemnon when he cries and announces that the Greeks should retreat. Besides, the Trojans are fighting for their homeland. The only honor they can achieve is to defend it to the end. Their choice is to die with honor or without it.

    Hector also must choose to fight Achilles. If he continues to run away or if he retreats behind the walls of Troy, he must live with the fact that he and his people will consider him a coward, and, in his society, most people cannot live without public approval. He could move to a different community and hope to start a new life there. However, his reputation would probably catch up with him, and even if he were successful, he would have to live with his own self-image. Hector must accept the fact that every human being faces death sooner or later. The question is not whether he will die, but how. The goal is to die a heroic death so that people will remember one's heroism.

19. **Achilles' use of the word "we."** Students' answers may vary. It could be the "royal we," meaning "I," except that Homer does not use that terminology. It could refer to Athena, because she helped Achilles by pretending to be Hector's brother. It could refer to Patroclus, whose death at the hands of Hector Achilles was obliged to repay in kind, so that Achilles killed Hector for both of them.

    It could conceivably refer to the other Greek warriors, to make them feel a part of the action and a part of the victory. This is a magnanimous attitude, and someone else might have said "we" with this intent, but it is out of character for Achilles to have had this in mind. He does not voluntarily perform one generous deed in the entire epic.

20. **Achilles' barbaric treatment of Hector.** Homer makes Achilles barbaric because he realizes that the line between a successful warrior and an animal is very thin. The qualities that make a warrior successful do not make him successful as a human being. The nature of war is inhumane, and it can make beasts of the participants.

21. **Live servant versus dead hero.** It is interesting to speculate whether Achilles would have remained in the Trojan War if he had realized the nature of death. He probably would have made the same choice, for the same reason that Hector did. If he had returned home, he would have had to spend the rest of his life living with at best an ordinary reputation and at worst the reputation of a coward. Once Hector killed Patroclus, Achilles no longer had a choice, no matter what the consequences. It was his obligation to kill Hector because Hector had killed his best friend.

22. **Paris.** Paris may be the most unusual person in *The Iliad*. He is not a man of his time, and he is in no way a Homeric hero.

It is quite in keeping with Paris's character that he stands upon the Trojan wall and kills Achilles from behind, instead of fighting him face to face. The bow was not a highly esteemed weapon by the Greeks. By its nature, a person used it to shoot animals or people from a distance. This obviously took less courage than the spear and the sword, which were used from a closer range.

Paris seems to be the only inner-motivated, conscienceless character in *The Iliad*. He does what he wants when he wants to do it, and it does not matter to him what anyone else thinks of his behavior. He does not mind that the Trojans hate him, and one can imagine the depth of their hatred. He feels no guilt that he is the cause of the war and that his people will be destroyed because of his lust. He remains remarkably good-natured, agreeing with Hector's criticism of him. He simply lives in a different world. He earns no respect in his world, and even we, who are much more inner-directed than these Greeks, are unlikely to respect him either. He is a completely selfish human being.

23. **Fairness of life.** *The Iliad* reflects that life is not fair, because people die regardless of whether or not they deserve to die. Hector dies even though he does his best to defend his country against invaders. Patroclus dies even though he does his best to make up for Achilles' intransigence. Paris lives even though he is the person who caused the war.

24. **Strength and weakness.** Each of the major characters in *The Iliad* has a tragic flaw in the sense that his greatest strength is his greatest weakness. Hector's greatest strength is his concern for what others will think of him. This motivates him to be the greatest of Trojan heroes. Yet he brings catastrophe to his warriors and death upon himself by not retreating when that is the intelligent course of action, because he is afraid that people will view him as a coward.

Patroclus's greatest strength is his desire to do his best. He undertakes to fight for Achilles. He continues to do his best on the battlefield even when he should have obeyed Achilles' advice and retreated. He cannot do less than his best; he cannot win less honor for himself in order to save more honor for Achilles. As a result, he is killed.

Achilles' and Agamemnon's greatest strength is their pride. They act as they do in order to win public approval and self-esteem. It is this great pride that causes them to argue and to mistreat each other. Neither is willing to recognize that the other is better in a particular way. As a result, their argument causes a disaster among the Greek forces.

Paris's greatest appeal must be his personality. His joy of living must be truly infectious. Under ordinary circumstances, he probably would bring joy and laughter with him wherever he went. In time of war, however, such a personality is a disaster.

25. **Behavior pattern.**

aretē (excellence):
a. Agamemnon: commander-in-chief of all the Greek forces
b. Achilles: greatest Greek fighter
c. Patroclus: great and enthusiastic fighter
d. Hector: commander of the Trojan forces and their greatest fighter

hubris (excessive pride):
a. Agamemnon: thinks he can do as he pleases because of his social and military rank
b. Achilles: thinks he can get his way because he is the greatest Greek fighter
c. Patroclus: thinks he can be of greater help to the Greeks than Achilles wants him to be because he is such a successful warrior
d. Hector: thinks he can stand up to Achilles because he is the greatest Trojan warrior and that he is obligated to do so as the commander of the Trojan forces

atē (rash or imprudent behavior):
a. Agamemnon: takes Briseis from Achilles
b. Achilles: withdraws from the war and refuses to accept Agamemnon's apology and gifts
c. Patroclus: pushes the Trojans back to their wall even though by so doing he knows that he is disobeying Achilles' orders
d. Hector: remains on the battlefield with the Trojan warriors after Achilles returns to battle instead of returning to the wall to fight as he is wisely advised to do

nemesis (retribution):
a. Agamemnon: is publicly humiliated and must apologize to Achilles in order to give the Greeks some hope of winning the war
b. Achilles: feels forced to send Patroclus into battle; as a result, when Patroclus is killed, he is forced to accept Agamemnon's apology and gifts and enter the battle in order to kill Hector
c. Patroclus: is killed by Apollo and the Trojans
d. Hector: is forced to confront Achilles; after running away, Athena lures him to fight Achilles, and he dies

26. **Personality changes.** Students' opinions may vary. It is possible that only Achilles' personality changes. After Patroclus dies, he loses the humanity he once had, treating Trojans like dogs and killing them. Earlier, he had made slaves of them instead. Some scholars feel that he learns more self-control, but his self-control with Priam is so fragile that one could find their argument unconvincing.

27. **Ending.** Homer ends *The Iliad* abruptly because he was interested only in a particular, narrow focus: the anger of Achilles and the disaster that that brought the Greeks. When Achilles comes to the end of his anger, which he

does when he returns Hector to Priam, Homer is finished. Thereafter, the disaster for the Greeks is also finished. They go on to win the war.

28. **Enriching lives of others.** Hector and Patroclus both live their lives in such a way that they enrich the lives of other people. Hector does his best to defend his people against the Greeks, and Patroclus does his best to save the Greek ships and drive the Trojans back to the Trojan wall. In contrast, when Achilles withdraws from battle with no regard for the cost to the Greeks, he fails to achieve this goal. Agamemnon also fails to achieve it, because his arrogance and pride cause the problem with Achilles. Enriching the lives of others is a good goal, because one of the most meaningful aspects of life is our relationships with other people.

29. **Heroic qualities.** Courage, skill in battle, and responsibility to one's community make a person heroic in *The Iliad.* Students' answers may vary. They may consider responsibility to one's community or nation a heroic value. Other possibilities are being good enough at sports or music to be famous; making important discoveries in science; helping nations get along with one another; venturing into outer space in order to further our knowledge.

30. **Achilles and Hector.** The basic similarities and differences between Achilles and Hector are discussed in the answers to questions 7–11, 15–20, and 24–25. Achilles is far more selfish, so Hector is a far better commander and a greater hero. However, both are motivated by winning the approval of others. Therefore, if Hector had had a commander who had taken away his prize of honor, he might also have withdrawn from battle as a protest. However, he probably would have accepted his commander's public apology and his gifts, whereas Achilles refuses to do so.

31. **Hector and Paris.** Hector and Paris are opposites and function as foils for one another. Hector is serious, responsive to the needs of his community and his obligation to his people, concerned with the opinions of others as a way of achieving self-esteem, and sensitive about how his actions will affect the future of his community. Paris is fun-loving and irresponsible, feeling no obligation to his people, and the opinions of others have no effect upon his self-esteem. He does not care at all what other people think of him, and he does not care how his actions affect the future of his community. Hector does his best to save Troy, whereas Paris does not care what happens to Troy. Hector is outer-motivated, whereas Paris is inner-motivated. Hector has a strong conscience, whereas Paris has no conscience at all.

32. **Paris and Helen.** Paris and Helen are more alike than they are different. Both are irresponsible and feel no obligation to their people. Helen may appear to be more serious than Paris, in that she talks as if she has a conscience, but her actions are as self-centered and short-sighted as those of Paris. Although Helen claims that the opinions of others have a devastating effect upon her self-esteem, she does nothing to win anyone's esteem. Like Paris, Helen does not care how her actions affect the future of her community, whether it is Greek or Trojan.

33. **Why Homer portrays only leaders.** Homer's audience was limited to aristocrats, who had little interest in tales about ordinary people. They wanted to hear about people like themselves. Many people in his audience had ancestors who had fought in the Trojan War, and they took great pride in their heritage. However, as far as we are concerned, the effect of the myth would be the same if these were ordinary people. In fact, it is because the characters think, speak, and act like ordinary people that we identify with them and value *The Iliad.*

34. **Homer's attitudes toward war.** (a) Agamemnon reveals how war can bring out an overwhelming need for personal power, even in those who already are great leaders. Whenever this happens, everyone suffers. Despite the fact that he is an experienced ruler, Agamemnon is unable to handle his responsibility to others in his new role as commander-in-chief of the Greek forces. Although he should not be an autocrat, he persists in seeing the war only in terms of his own self-interest. Consequently, instead of being a leader among warriors, he participates in the war in a way that will best preserve his own life. Moreover, instead of treating his leaders in a way that will enable a united Greek force to win the war, his treatment of Achilles divides, demoralizes, and weakens the Greeks, thereby causing great injury and loss of life among the men under his command. (b) Achilles reveals how war can remove the civilized veneer from any warrior, even the greatest of heroes, and substitute an underlying heart of darkness in its place. Between Patroclus's death and his meeting with Priam, Achilles loses his humanity. By permitting himself to be ruled by his passions, he reduces himself to a kind of death-machine. Achilles' behavior causes readers to shudder at the capacity for evil that is part of human nature and to reevaluate Achilles both as a civilized human being and as a hero. (c) Patroclus reveals how war can inspire men to become heroes, even if their heroism causes their death. Patroclus's success in battle fires his spirit, giving him the courage to tackle all adversaries, including Apollo himself. His behavior is self-defeating to the extent that it causes his death, but he saves the Greeks and earns the immortality of lasting fame. (d) Through Hector, Homer reveals the fact that war robs civilization of its best people, as well as a multitude of innocent men, women, and children. By depicting the Trojans as ordinary human beings, rather than as villains, Homer reveals the real tragedy of war: its overwhelming and indiscriminate destruction of human life. Hector, in a courageous but very human way, fights what he knows is a losing battle against the Greeks, doing his best to preserve the life of his people for as long as possible. Yet even he lets his success on the battlefield cloud his good judgment. After he kills Patroclus, he rejects the sensible advice to fight from the wall, and by unnecessarily exposing his men, he causes more of them to become wounded and killed in battle. Hector's courage in facing certain death after having unsuccessfully run from Achilles around the wall of Troy reveals how war can bring out the best in a human being. Hector, the greatest of the Trojan warriors, dies an even greater man. (e) Through the character of Paris, Homer depicts the ability of people to be indifferent

to the tragedy of war, even when they are confronted by it, know that they are responsible for it, and expect that it will overwhelm them. Unlike Achilles, who acts on principle and tries to foresee the consequences of his actions, Paris puts frivolous personal desires before those of his family and community. Because Paris's abduction of Helen has caused the war, his indifference to more than nine years of massive injury and death, to the impending disaster that hovers over his city and his people, and to criticism from any source is despicable. Consequently, Paris's character causes readers to question the role of the Trojans in this war. Their tolerance of Paris brings their destruction upon them. In the words of a famous saying, "All it takes for evil to triumph is for good men to stand by and do nothing." (f) Through Andromache, Homer depicts the female victims of war. Like other women of royal blood, Andromache will be given to one of the victors as a prize of honor and will be forced to leave her homeland in order to begin life as a slave in a new country. Based upon her knowledge of the similar plight of other women, she foresees that her royalty will do little more than preserve her life for awhile. (g) Through the character of Helen, Homer reveals war to be an unmitigated tragedy. In one respect, the idea that many nations would fight a ten-year war on foreign soil in order to recapture a woman testifies to the importance of women in their society. However, Homer's Helen is not worth even one battle. It is not clear whether she went with Paris willingly or unwillingly; she blames Aphrodite. She remains with Paris in Troy even though she does not respect him and recognizes that her behavior is disastrous to Greeks and Trojans alike. She helps the Greeks in one situation (Odysseus's spying mission), yet does her best to trick them in another (when the Greeks are hiding within the wooden horse). In a comic setting, Helen's personality would be a source of great humor, but this is war.

35. **The gods' participation in war.** The Greek gods participate in the Trojan War at least partly because it was the poetic convention in Homer's time to have them play an important role. Before Homer's time, the gods represented all the forces active in the life experience that the Greeks could explain in no other way. For example, early Greeks thought that the gods caused changes in weather, illness, and both good and bad luck. The early Greeks also believed that the gods gave human beings both good and bad ideas and whatever skills they possessed. Homer is inconsistent in his depiction of the powers of the gods, often having them behave like young children, and often having his human characters take responsibility for their own thoughts and actions.

　　The mythological cause of this war is the awarding of the golden apple to Aphrodite, who rewards Paris with Helen. Thus, three goddesses cause and perpetuate the war because of their fragile egos. They are as arrogant, proud, and self-centered as Agamemnon and Achilles. Yet, the cause of the Trojan War concerns Homer as little as the cause of the argument between Achilles and Agamemnon does. Homer is preoccupied with human beings and how they react in times of great stress. He even uses the gods to sharpen his focus on the human beings who interest him.

36. **Gods representing forces.** Students' answers may vary. Some examples include: (a) nature: Aphrodite creates a dense mist in order to hide Paris; Apollo causes the plague that afflicts the Greeks; (b) human thought: Athena tells Achilles to fight Agamemnon with words instead of with his sword; Athena convinces Pandarus to break the truce; (c) human skill: Apollo weakens Patroclus, enabling the Trojans to kill him; (d) luck: Aphrodite causes Paris's helmet strap to break so that she can rescue him.

One incident that can only be explained as divine action occurs when Athena appears as Deiphobus, gives Hector the courage to fight Achilles, and then disappears.

37. **Achilles' choice.** Students' responses will vary.

38. **Values today.** Dignity and pride are still very important today because we value self-respect very highly. People try to achieve honor, glory, and fame. Honor is the easiest to achieve because our society rewards those who perform their jobs unusually well. People may be promoted or earn special kinds of vacations or be praised at dinners and assemblies. Glory is earned primarily on the battlefield, at the frontiers of science, and in the sports arena. Television and movie stars, athletes, and musicians earn fame. Revenge is no longer an important value. Courts of law determine justice instead of leaving it to be decided as an individual chooses.

39. **Homer's similes.** Homer's similes describe: natural phenomena, such as mists, waves, forest fires, and the flight of birds; hunting scenes, where an animal is cornered; pastoral scenes, such as boys playing in the country and activities on the farm. The similes describe life in Homer's time, where people were close to nature in many of their daily pursuits. The similes dramatize comparisons, thus intensifying the emotion being described.

JASON AND THE GOLDEN FLEECE (PAGE 159)

1. **Pelias and *aretē, hubris, atē,* and *nemesis.*** Pelias is so powerful and successful (his areas of excellence, or *aretē*) that he thinks he should be king of Iolcus (his excessive pride, or *hubris*) instead of Aeson, his half-brother. Therefore, Pelias takes the kingdom from Aeson (his blind, reckless behavior, or *atē*). Jason is obligated to restore his father's kingdom (Pelias's retribution, or *nemesis*). However, before Jason can do this, Pelias sends Jason on a journey that Pelias expects will kill him (another form of *atē*). Not long thereafter, when Pelias thinks that Jason is dead, Pelias will be responsible for Aeson's death (still another form of *atē*). Then Jason will be obligated to kill Pelias (Pelias's retribution, or *nemesis*).

2. **Jason's encounters with Pelias.** Jason's first meeting with Pelias reveals Jason to be a man of words. His speech is conciliatory but firm. Pelias may keep the wealth that he unjustly took from Aeson, Jason's father, but he must return the symbols of kingship and the kingdom. It is important to note that Jason makes no attempt to threaten Pelias.

Later, when Pelias solicits Jason's response to his "theoretical" problem, Jason reacts as if Pelias is not trying to trick him. However, still later, it is clear that Jason suspects Pelias's true motives because, after he sees that Acastus and the shipbuilder will sail with him, Jason states that Pelias may not have intended to kill him after all. However, Jason is not daunted by the risk, and he shows no fear. Acquiring the Golden Fleece is a heroic task, and he wishes to gain lasting fame. By emphasizing the risk to Pelias, he encourages Pelias to send him on the quest.

3. **Why Jason suggests the quest to Pelias.** It is characteristic of young adults that they view themselves as invulnerable and immortal. Therefore, Jason's desire to achieve the glory of the great deed and the lasting fame that it brings outweighs any fear of failure and death. Moreover, Jason risks losing his life if he remains in Iolcus. He knows that Pelias would never choose to return his kingdom to Aeson. Jason's only choice is to collect an army and hope to defeat Pelias and his warriors in battle, which Jason is in no position to do since Pelias is such a powerful king.

   It is possible to attribute Jason's suggestion to Hera, who belatedly claims responsibility for it. However, Jason has his own reasons for making the suggestion, and the fact that he is ambitious enough to do it will be supported by the rest of this myth.

4. **Phineus's behavior and *aretē, hubris, atē,* and *nemesis.*** Phineus warns Jason and the Argonauts about the pattern in human behavior that involves *aretē* (excellence), *hubris* (excessive pride), *atē* (blind, reckless behavior), and *nemesis* (retribution). Phineus's gift of prophecy from Apollo is his *aretē.* Phineus's ability to know everything that is to come made him think that it was his gift to mortals—even his obligation to them—to tell them all that he knew (*hubris*). Therefore, Phineus told all (*atē*), and by so doing, he acted as if he were Apollo himself, rather than a mortal king who was subject to the rule of the Olympian gods. In response, Zeus punished Phineus by blinding him (Phineus's *nemesis*) and afflicting him with his hounds, the Harpies.

5. **Role of Eros's arrows.** Eros's arrows symbolize "love at first sight." Because they control the emotional response of whomever they hit, they represent the irrational nature of love—the fact that a person feels unable to control his or her emotional response to the love object and therefore feels helpless. Even the gods fear Eros's arrows because once Eros hits his target, that person—god or mortal—will fall in love with the next living thing she or he sees. The object of passionate desire may be divine, mortal, animal, or vegetable. Therefore, the consequences can be very embarrassing.

6. **Aeetes' palace and behavior.** King Aeetes' palace reveals him to be the son of Helios, god of the sun. Therefore, he has unusual power and unusual skill, and, in fact, he is immortal. Being more important than Jason, Aeetes will expect to have his way. He is not likely to be influenced by the honeyed words of a stranger from Hellas.

   Although host-gifts are customary and important, a king would not give his most prized possession as a host-gift to a stranger whose father is unknown. Therefore, Aeetes does not suffer from *hubris* (excessive pride), and his refusal is not a form of *atē* (blind, reckless behavior).

Aeetes has no reason to expect that Jason will cheat in order to win the fleece, and he has no reason to expect that his daughter will commit treason in order to help him. Consequently, Aeetes is totally unprepared for what happens. One can consider his loss of a daughter and the death of his son a form of retribution for his refusal to give up the fleece peacefully, but this is not divine retribution. It is caused by two people (Jason and Medea) who behave dishonorably.

7. **Jason's acceptance of Aeetes' tasks.** Jason does not accept Aeetes' guarantee of safe passage from Aea because it would be humiliating to do so. He has come for the Golden Fleece. To leave without making his best effort to acquire it would bring him shame in the eyes of his heroic companions. No doubt Aeetes would ridicule him as well. However, since Aeetes is a stranger from a distant culture, what Aeetes thinks of Jason probably would be less important than what the Argonauts think of him. Therefore, Jason has no choice but to accept Aeetes' plan. His decision marks him as a man of character and a hero. It will be the manner in which he performs these tasks that, arguably, tarnishes both his character and his heroism.

8. **Peleus vs. Jason.** Just as, earlier, Jason handles King Pelias diplomatically, now, in preparing to meet King Aeetes and win the Golden Fleece, Jason once again intends to use honeyed words instead of threats of action. This attitude is typical of how Jason handles problems. He is a man of words, not deeds, and he is accustomed to convincing others to help him accomplish his goals.

In contrast, Peleus is the traditional hero. He is a man of courage, strength, and skill. He is always prepared to fight for what he wants, and he encourages the Argonauts to be confident in their own courage, strength, and skill on the plain of battle. Peleus appears to be more heroic than Jason because he is a courageous man of action, and he will accomplish great deeds without help from others. However, Jason possesses the social skills that bring advancement in society, both in time of peace and, if a commander-in-chief is necessary, in time of war as well.

Not long thereafter, Jason accepts Aeetes' tasks even though he knows that he cannot perform them. He returns to the Argonauts overwhelmed with despair. In contrast, Peleus announces that he will perform these tasks in Jason's place. He gives the following rationale, which is the attitude of the traditional hero: Death awaits heroes and cowards alike, so it is best to live and die with honor. Here, Peleus is clearly the greater hero because he has the courage to fight when it is necessary. Moreover, it would not occur to him to ask for help or to cheat in order to accomplish this goal.

9. **Jason's attitude.** This is a difficult question because, in real life, heroes do lie, cheat, and steal under certain circumstances, such as in time of war, when all civilized values are suspended and any means justifies the end. Their only excuses are that they are acting on behalf of their country, and that such behavior is expected of them.

In contrast, Jason is acting on his own behalf. He may, in the process, bring glory to Hellas, but the quest is personal. It is King Pelias's way of killing him, and Jason knows it. The peculiarly Greek aspect of Jason's situation is that he loses either way. He cannot survive without cheating because that is the only way that he can hope to perform these tasks. It would be unacceptably humiliating to permit Peleus to perform the tasks for him.

However, heroism involves honor as well as courage, strength, and skill. Therefore, what Jason is supposed to do is just what Peleus would do—die heroically in the process of trying to perform his tasks. Jason is unwilling to risk his life in order to get the fleece. In this sense, he is a coward, and he lacks the virtues of the traditional Greek hero.

In contrast, later heroes are often valued more for their ability to relate well to others and adapt to circumstances than for their inflexible individualism. Therefore, while Jason is not a traditional hero, it is possible to interpret his behavior as pragmatic and prudent in that he does whatever he can do well, but he delegates to others whatever they can do better than he. For example, he gives the sons of Boreas permission to save Phineus by attacking the Harpies.

Jason's excellence, or *aretē,* is his leadership ability—his ability to speak and act in such an appealing manner that others will help him attain a particular goal or set of goals. Jason suffers from excessive pride (*hubris*) in that he thinks his goals are worth whatever means will accomplish them, no matter what the cost to others. Therefore, he has no qualms about asking Medea to become a traitor to her family and her people on his behalf. This is blind and reckless behavior (*atē*) in that Jason is blind to the true nature of his deed and, therefore, blind to the consequences that will surely follow. However, the retribution (*nemesis*) that Jason eventually receives appears years later. The immediate consequences are that he becomes ever more dependent on Medea in order to survive, and he becomes increasingly less heroic as he asks, or permits, her to act on his behalf.

10. **Jason vs. Heracles and Odysseus/Ulysses.** In most Western societies, the traditional hero is male. In myth, Odysseus is depicted from two points of view. To Homer's Greek warriors, he is a great hero. However, in *The Aeneid*—where he is called Ulysses—he is a great enemy of the Trojans.

The traditional hero does his best to live so as to achieve the glory of the great deed, which, in turn, will bring him lasting fame. Heracles, Odysseus/Ulysses, and Jason all conform to this mold. Most traditional heroes have a strong desire to serve the needs of their community—such as by destroying an animal or monster that is damaging the food supply and bringing death to people and livestock. Heracles' labors perform this function. Odysseus participates in the Trojan War in order to honor his—and therefore his community's—obligation to King Menelaus of Sparta. His participation enables the warriors of his community to take their place among the warriors of the other important Greek communities and, thus, to achieve Hellenic identity and pride by being part of a major Greek offensive against an offending, non-Greek community. To these Hellenic warriors, to be praised by their peers is one of the principal factors that motivates and governs their behavior.

In contrast, Jason is not responding to the needs of his community. Whereas the other Argonauts choose to accompany Jason in order to enhance their identity and pride as Hellenes, Jason cares only about the success of his quest and the fame that it will bring him.

The traditional hero must go on a quest. Heracles must bring King Eurystheus the skin of the Nemean lion, Artemis's sacred deer, the Erymanthian boar, the Cretan bull, King Diomedes' mares, Queen Hippolyte's belt, Geryon's cattle, the Hesperides' golden apples, and Hades' guard-dog, Cerberus. Odysseus/Ulysses must capture Helen of Troy and return her to King Menelaus of Sparta. Jason must bring King Pelias the Golden Fleece.

However, the traditional hero is an individualist. He acts alone, and his major accomplishments are his own. In contrast, Jason's two principal tasks, or labors, involve manipulating other people so that they will enable him to accomplish his quest. First, Jason must arrange to have a company of heroic individuals work together in order to achieve its common goal, the success of the *Argo*'s voyage. Then, Jason must persuade Medea to give him the help that will enable him to perform the tasks that Aeetes demands of him and that will enable him to acquire the Golden Fleece. Without the help of the Argonauts and Medea, Jason will fail.

The traditional hero possesses courage, strength, and skill. He uses his particular skill, at which he is superb (his *aretē*), in order to perform the necessary tasks or labors that will enable him to succeed in accomplishing the object of his quest. Heracles' *aretē* is his prodigious strength combined with his creative intelligence. Although he is famous for his might, Heracles must use his brain as well as his brawn in order to succeed with his tasks. Odysseus/Ulysses' *aretē* are his scheming mind and his ability to use words in order to accomplish his schemes.

In contrast, Jason lacks self-confidence, great physical strength, and skill in battle. His *aretē* is his leadership ability—his ability to speak and act in such an appealing manner that others will help him attain a particular goal or set of goals. Once Jason succeeds in winning Medea, she uses her skill with drugs to give him the strength and skill that he lacks. Moreover, either Medea must continue to give Jason the courage that he needs if he is going to succeed, or she must perform the deed herself. (Note (a) Jason's behavior and Medea's continued prompting when Jason must confront the earth-born, bronze-clad warriors; and (b) Medea's need to put the serpent to sleep and advise Jason about taking the Golden Fleece from the tree on which it hangs.)

It is important to understand the difference between Odysseus/Ulysses and Jason. Odysseus is a courageous and skillful warrior who is renowned for his creative intelligence. Homer calls him "the man of many wiles." Like Odysseus, Jason is a gifted speaker, and, like Odysseus, he speaks and acts so as to persuade others to comply with his wishes. In contrast, Jason does not have Odysseus's clever intelligence. Whereas Odysseus is "a man of many schemes," Jason is a man of no schemes at all. Jason uses his appealing words and manner in order to get others to give him the help—including the schemes—that he needs.

Finally, the traditional hero is a man of honor. Heracles and Odysseus/Ulysses perform their tasks in ways that are consistent with the heroic code and that are acceptable to the person who has assigned them. When Heracles receives help or payment, Eurystheus demands that he perform two additional labors. When Odysseus is deceptive in the course of the Trojan War, his behavior is acceptable because it is part of a necessary role that will benefit all of the Greek warriors.

In contrast, Jason is not a man of honor, but a man of excessive ambition, expedience, and total self-interest. His excellence, or *aretē,* is his leadership ability—his ability to speak and act in such an appealing manner that others will help him attain a particular goal or set of goals. However, Jason suffers from excessive pride (*hubris*) in that he thinks his goals are worth whatever means will accomplish them, and he does not concern himself with the cost to others of his demands. Therefore, Jason has no qualms about asking Medea to use her skills to enable him to perform the tasks that her father is demanding of him—even though, by acting on Jason's behalf, Medea will betray her father and her people. Later, when meeting Aeetes in battle appears to mean certain death, Jason has no qualms about asking Medea to sacrifice her brother's life on his behalf. Moreover, unlike the traditional hero, Jason feels no compelling need to perform heroic deeds himself. Therefore, he has no qualms about having Medea put the serpent that guards the Golden Fleece to sleep and then tell him how to remove the fleece from the oak tree on which it hangs.

11. **Medea's decision to help Jason.** Medea decides to help Jason because she has fallen in love with him, she wants to prevent his death, and she thinks that she is the only person who can save him from her father. Her emotion is really infatuation, rather than love, since Medea knows nothing about Jason's character and does not know if Jason will reciprocate her love. Clearly, she is acting purely out of passion. Every aspect of common sense would be against her attitudes and behavior. She has too much to lose, and she has no idea of what she will gain.

Medea is suffering from the behavior pattern that Phineus earlier describes to the Argonauts. Her *aretē* is her skill with herbs and drugs. She suffers from *hubris* in that she thinks that she is the only person who can help Jason, and that, if she doesn't, he will die. Actually, it is the role of Jason's heroic companions to help him, and he has a whole shipload of them. Medea's actual help is reckless, and, although she foresees the consequences, it is blind (*atē*) because she helps Jason without knowing the true nature of his character. Medea is blinded by Jason's form and face, and by his honeyed words. For Medea, retribution (*nemesis*) comes in the form of her need to cut herself off permanently from her family and her country and, in their place, to have to depend totally on the kindness of a stranger.

12. **Good and evil in disguise.** Phineus tells the Argonauts that good and evil can appear in disguise. Both Jason (unknowingly) and Medea (knowingly) are experiencing this fact. It appears to Jason to be acceptable—and, in fact, good—that Medea will use her special powers to help him perform the tasks that Aeetes demands of him and to help him acquire the Golden Fleece. Jason does not view this as cheating, and it does not bother him that Medea is committing treason on his behalf. In contrast, Medea understands the treacherous nature of her help, but she acts out of love for a stranger—unaware that his character is not what it appears to be.

13. **Significance of Medea's dream.** Medea's dream reveals the depth of her love for Jason in that it reveals her subconscious wish to marry Jason and return to Hellas with him, despite the break with her family that this decision will create. (Her dream could not reveal Jason's wishes because he and Medea have not spoken; they have only looked at each other from a distance.)

Medea's dream also reflects reality. It foreshadows the future in that, in a very real sense, Medea, rather than Jason, will be performing all of Jason's tasks. Her skill with magic, which enables her to perform these tasks so easily in her dream, will actually enable Jason to perform them easily.

Medea's dream also reflects reality in that she knows her father well enough to anticipate all of his reactions to what will come to pass. Aeetes will know that Jason never would have been able to perform these tasks without Medea's help. Therefore, he will refuse to give up the Golden Fleece. Finally, Medea will have to choose between her father and Jason. She will choose Jason, and her choice will cause her family the anguish and anger that she anticipates.

14. **Medea's manipulation of Chalciope.** Medea manipulates Chalciope by telling her that she dreamed that their father killed Chalciope's sons. Although Medea did not dream this, she knows her father well enough to know that this is just what he intends to do, given their role in Jason's life. What Medea gains is Chalciope's plea to save her sons. This gives Medea tacit permission to do what she wants to do, which is to help Jason. It turns her deed from a selfish one to a selfless one, and, in her mind, it ameliorates the treachery that is involved since she will be helping her sister.

15. **Irony of Helios's prophecy.** Helios's ambiguous prophecy is ironic because Aeetes misinterprets it. Aeetes is positive that the deceitful schemes that will lead to treachery and destruction will come from the sons of Phrixus. It never occurs to him that Medea will be the traitor. The decisions are Jason's and Medea's. However, the sons of Phrixus are indirectly and partially responsible for what happens in that they persuade Jason to ask for Medea's help.

16. **Medea's vacillation and decision.** Medea's vacillation is very realistic, and it makes her a very sympathetic character. She knows that she has vowed to perform a treacherous act—one that will sever her ties to her family. Yet, she sees no way to avoid inevitable suffering. Medea decides against suicide because it is natural that a maiden in love would want to live, not die. Continued life

offers everything to Medea except her parents, while death offers nothing. Medea's response also makes psychological sense in that she is ruled by her passions. Therefore, her passionate love for Jason will lead her to resolve all internal conflicts in his favor.

17. **Jason's persuasion of Medea.** Golden-tongued Jason is doing what he does best! Note the levels on which he appeals: lovely maiden; have no fear; you are kind; you have the power to help me; you have promised to help me; I invoke the gods as I ask for your help; your power will save me, or I will die; without your help, all my companions will die, too; if you help me, you will gain great and broad fame; everyone will praise you.

18. **Medea's rejuvenation of Jason.** Medea's unusual ability to restore the dead to life and youth must be viewed as a form of foreshadowing. Having done this once, Medea can choose to do it again. Moreover, under different circumstances, she might contrive to have different results.

19. **Medea's thoughts versus Jason's.** Jason's golden tongue leads Medea to believe that she now has what she wants, Jason's love. Therefore, she puts herself and her future into his hands. In contrast, after his loving speech, Jason's thoughts return immediately to the business at hand. They must separate lest someone find them together and thus spoil their plan. Also, Medea must flee with Apsyrtus. This contrast reveals Medea to be very much in love, whereas Jason is expressing a love that he does not feel or, at best, a love that differs markedly in quality from Medea's love.

Once they have separated, Jason is joyful because he has acquired what he wants, which is Medea's help. Note that, once again, he has achieved what he wants by using honeyed words. In contrast, Medea is torn between her love for Jason and the destruction that her love is going to create. She realizes that, by giving Jason the drugs he needs, she has now passed the point of no return. She has forsaken her parents and homeland, and she has cast her lot with a stranger from a strange land. She has traded a life of innocence and joy for a life of anxiety and guilt.

This contrast reveals Jason to be a selfish manipulator, who will do anything—including promise anything—to get what he wants. It reveals Medea to be a tragic figure, who has let her passion stifle her reason and who will begin to suffer dreadful consequences.

20. **Jason's words about Apsyrtus.** Jason's words suggest that, at some future point, Apsyrtus will have to be murdered. When, where, and by whom (Jason or Medea) is not clear. However, Jason explains the reason. It is possible that he does not use Apsyrtus's name because he does not know it. However, to refer to the boy as "your brother" depersonalizes him and will make it easier to murder him.

21. **Hera's character.** Hera's joy that, through Medea, Jason will capture the Golden Fleece and she (Hera) will avenge Pelias's insult to her honor reveals that Hera is similar to Jason in that she apparently will do whatever is necessary in order to achieve her goal (to punish Pelias), no matter who is hurt (or

killed) in the process. This reveals Hera to be a goddess who revels in her power and who cares only about how others (both gods and mortals) treat her.

Although Hera's nature is human rather than godlike, it can be viewed as being irrelevant to this story. Each character's thoughts and actions are true to the nature of that character's particular personality and true to what is potential in human nature.

22. **Analysis of similes.** Homeric similes enhance the character(s) they describe. Their lengthy detail enables them to be unusually effective because they call forth a scene in which a similar action is occurring. The following similes compare their subjects to aspects of life in ancient times: war; metalwork; and country life. Examples of these similes include (a) comparing Jason to a war horse that is longing for battle; (b) comparing Aeetes' bulls to a blacksmith working his bellows; and (c) comparing the earth-born warriors to mountain streams flooding in the spring and to a pack of hungry wolves breaking into a sheepfold.

The shorter similes are also picturesque. To a lesser extent, they add dimension to what a character is doing. The following similes all compare their subjects to aspects of nature: (a) comparing Jason to summer lightning; (b) comparing the bulls' breath to storm winds and their hooves to lightning; (c) comparing the earth-born warriors to storm winds and great oak trees; (d) comparing Jason to a fiery comet; and (e) comparing the earth-born warriors to stalks of grain beneath a farmer's sickle.

23. **Jason as he performs his tasks.** Unlike the traditional hero, Jason is fearful as he performs his tasks. For example, he constantly turns around in order to be certain that he is safe from the earth-born warriors. Medea's voice must urge him repeatedly to toss the boulder among the warriors. After he finally throws the boulder, he hides behind his shield so the earth-born warriors will not see him.

The question is whether Jason is less heroic because of his fear or more heroic because he conquers his fear. Actually, fear is a sensible, self-protective reaction to a dangerous situation, and a hero's fear may reveal how dangerous a particular situation is. Therefore, the hero who conquers his fear is often considered to be more heroic than the hero who goes forth as if no danger exists. However, in myth, the traditional hero is so self-confident of his strength and skill that he is only afraid when he knows that he is vulnerable and, therefore, about to die.

Aeetes demands that Jason perform the type of tasks that the traditional hero performs. However, Jason is not a traditional hero, and he knows it. In contrast, he is more pragmatic and prudent in that he does whatever he can do well, but he always delegates to others whatever they can do better than he. Ironically, Jason has encouraged Medea to give him the physical strength and skill of a traditional hero, but he cannot muster the traditional hero's self-confidence. Psychologically, Jason cannot help but think of himself as "a fish out of water," and therefore, without Medea's prodding, he cannot trust her gifts. Consequently, he often thinks and acts like a coward as he performs these tasks.

24. **Medea's reaction to her treachery.** Medea's reaction to her treachery is psychologically realistic. By letting her emotions guide her behavior, what she has most feared has come to pass. The natural question is what to do, and both suicide and flight are options. Moreover, most people would shun death and choose to flee.

25. **Why Medea now calls Jason by his name.** The term "stranger" implies formality and distance. Therefore, Medea's use of Jason's name now marks a major change in their relationship. Jason has now replaced Medea's father as her protector, and therefore, from this time forth, it is Jason who must see that other people respect and honor her. Medea's use of Jason's name reflects her dependence on Jason and the closer nature of their new relationship.

26. **Jason's priorities.** Jason repeats his declaration of love, but now his commitment is more obligatory because he swears a sacred oath before Zeus and Hera that he will love and protect Medea forever. He follows this oath immediately with comments about Apsyrtus, almost as if the oath were not important. This foreshadows the time, in the following myth (*Medea*), when Jason will disregard it. Jason ought to know that such an oath is unbreakable. Therefore, he should have taken care to avoid making a sacred promise that he may be unwilling to keep.

    For the first time, Jason now mentions that they will only be safe once Apsyrtus is dead. He is astute enough to know that, had he mentioned it earlier, Medea might have taken back her drugs and refused to help him. Now that the treacherous deed has occurred, Medea no longer has a choice, and Jason knows that it is safe to be honest about her brother.

    When Medea is outraged, Jason smoothly changes the focus from controversy to achieving his final goal, acquiring the Golden Fleece. This reveals how shallow, self-serving, and callous he is. No matter what sweet words flow from his mouth, he is using Medea to achieve his personal goals. She is currently necessary, and in order to get what he wants from her, he will lie by omission, if necessary, and he will change the subject, if necessary. Medea's situation and her feelings are not important to Jason, and, therefore, he will not deal with them.

27. **Jason and Medea versus the serpent.** Just as Jason had the thoughts and behavior of a coward while dealing with the earth-born warriors, so, now, he is terrified of the serpent that guards the Golden Fleece. He keeps his distance and remains behind Medea; in fact, it takes all his courage just to remain nearby.

    Jason's behavior confirms the fearsome nature of the serpent. Moreover, his behavior is consistent with the nature of his character in that here he is behaving prudently under the circumstances. Jason always knows his physical limitations, and he always respects them. He knows that he is not one of the great traditional heroes, like Heracles, and therefore that he lacks the power to deal with this immortal creature. Consequently, once again, Jason is pragmatic in that he delegates to others whatever they can do better than he. Here Medea possesses both the magic to lull the serpent to sleep and the knowledge to direct Jason in his removal of the fleece. Therefore, Jason retreats and lets Medea help him.

28. **Medea's attitude toward Jason.** Jason loves the Golden Fleece in the way that Medea loves Jason. Moreover, Medea fears the loss of Jason just as Jason fears the loss of the fleece. Jason has done whatever was necessary in order to acquire the fleece, while Medea has done whatever was necessary in order to acquire Jason. Jason loves an object. The only person he appears to be capable of loving is himself. Medea's love, therefore, is not reciprocated, and given what she has sacrificed, this foreshadows serious trouble between them.

   It is ironic that Jason celebrates his acquisition of the Golden Fleece as if he is the person who won it. It is ironic that Jason compares himself with Heracles. Finally, it is ironic that someone who thinks of himself as Heracles should clutch the fleece in fear that someone will take it from him. Jason's ability to forget the circumstances of his victories and the fact that he has the *hubris* (excessive pride) to compare himself with Heracles confirm the nature of his character. These would be astounding if they were not two more examples of what type of person Jason is. His fear is a third example.

29. **Jason's speech to the Argonauts.** Jason's speech to the Argonauts reflects his *aretē* (excellence) as the leader of his expedition. Whereas his fear and weakness often cause Peleus to speak competitively as the real hero, here Jason is doing what he does best—speaking honeyed words in order to achieve his goals. He exudes gracious gratitude because he must explain Medea's presence on the return voyage in a way that respects them both. He must exert psychological leadership because, given the great threat that Aeetes presents, Jason must prepare his men for battle.

30. **Responsibility for Jason's success.** Jason is responsible for his success in that, first, he takes Argus's advice and permits Medea to help him; then he performs the tasks that Aeetes demands of him. Although it is Medea who makes it possible for him to succeed, he, and not she, must actually perform the tasks, and Jason could have been too afraid to try. However, Jason does not acquire the Golden Fleece.

   Medea is responsible for Jason's success in that, first, she gives him the herbs that will protect him from harm, and she rejuvenates him; then her voice reminds Jason of what he must do and tells him that he is able to do it; third, she puts the serpent to sleep and tells Jason how to remove the fleece from the tree on which it hangs; and finally, she agrees to the murder of her brother so that they can escape (with the fleece) from her father. Therefore, most readers will decide that Medea is more responsible than Jason for Jason's success.

31. **Contribution of Jason's physical appearance.** Jason's godlike appearance makes others either admire or fear him. It leads the Argonauts to respond to his invitation because it appears that the gods favor such a mortal and will

favor his quest. It leads them to choose Jason to lead them. "You can't judge a book by its cover," but first impressions give those who are attractive the benefit of the doubt. Moreover, Jason's appearance is part of his charm, and he uses the impression he makes to help him get others to carry out his wishes. Because of his physical beauty and his gift with words, Jason has no need to develop his courage, his physical strength, and his battle skills. He learns that he can persuade the other Argonauts and Medea to take risks for him.

If Jason had been short and homely, he would have to have developed compensatory qualities, such as remarkable intelligence, sensitivity, or loyalty. Odysseus/Ulysses was short and not particularly attractive, but his creative intelligence led him to be valued as one of the greatest of leaders to the Greeks and one of the most detested of enemies to the Trojans in the Trojan War.

32. **Jason as human being and hero.** Jason is ruled by unbridled ambition; therefore, he is opportunistic and pragmatic. He will pay any price for success, and he does not hesitate to use Medea in order to succeed in his quest for the Golden Fleece. For example: (a) Jason knows that he can be charming and that his success depends on the willingness of a young maiden to help him. Therefore, he turns on the charm. He has no qualms about using sweet words in order to persuade Medea to help him even though he knows that, by doing so, she will become a traitor to her father and her country. (b) Jason also has no qualms about cheating in order to perform the tasks that Medea's father is demanding of him. (c) Jason has no qualms about permitting Medea to lull the serpent to sleep so that he can collect the Golden Fleece even though, by doing so, it is she—rather than he—who actually captures it.

The nature of Jason's character affects the quality of his heroism in that he uses Medea to achieve his goals even though it will be only through her extensive help that he will capture the Golden Fleece and thus win the glory that brings lasting fame. Therefore, readers who consider heroism only in terms of the traditional hero will neither respect Jason's character nor value his deeds. However, other readers may appreciate Jason's ability to be pragmatic and prudent, and they may value Jason's ability to succeed by delegating to Medea whatever she can do better than he.

33. **The nature of Jason's success.** Jason's success is based on: his use of his charm; the nature of Medea's love for him; Medea's skillful use of herbs; and Medea's treachery. Therefore, Jason learns that personal goals are more important than one's responsibility to others, and he learns that charm, love, knowledge, and treachery are useful ways to attain the glory of the great deed.

However, Jason fails to learn that character is destiny. Success that has been based on these values is short-lived and hollow because ambition's tools damage the character of the ambitious woman or man. The first to fall are integrity and honor; without them, the structure of heroism and the respect of others collapses.

34. **Significance of the gods in the lives of Jason and Medea.** First, Aphrodite's role in Medea's life is to make her fall in love with Jason. Therefore, the goddess prevails upon Eros to accomplish this with his love-inspiring arrow. However, Medea is a young maiden, and Jason is a handsome hero. Therefore, it is natural that Medea might become infatuated with Jason and that the irrational nature of love would be revealed in the priority that Medea makes of her passion for Jason and in the sacrifices that follow.

Zeus's response to Jason's prayer reveals that the Olympian gods exist, that they listen to the prayers of human beings, and that they respond. In this instance, Zeus responds favorably. Therefore, Jason, the Argonauts, and the community can assume that the gods will protect Jason and his crew and that they will return home safely to Hellas.

Zeus's punishment of Phineus reveals a universe in which the gods demand certain types of behavior from human beings and punish those who oppose their will. Zeus will tolerate no competition from mortals. Human beings must realize that they are not divine, and they may not behave as if they are.

In contrast, Hera's role in the lives of Jason and Medea is debatable. After Jason responds to Pelias's "theoretical" problem, Hera declares that she has manipulated Jason's response. However, her timing reveals that she may be taking credit for Jason's independent response. Moreover, Jason's response is psychologically consistent with his personal goals.

Hera once again claims responsibility, after the fact, for the honeyed words that Jason uses in order to persuade Medea to help him. However, Jason has no need for Hera to put sweet and clever words into his mouth. Jason's golden tongue is his *aretē*. Given his hopeless situation and his *aretē*, it is natural that he would speak to Medea as he does.

When Hera also takes credit for Medea's refusal to commit suicide, the belated timing of the goddess's announcement reveals that she may be taking credit for Medea's independent response. Medea decides against suicide because it is natural that a maiden in love would want to live, not die. Medea's response is also psychologically consistent with her passionate nature and her love for Jason.

Consequently, the question of whether Jason and Medea have control over their own lives or whether they are the puppets or pawns of the gods is always debatable. Certainly, it is possible to view both Medea and Jason as the helpless victims of the amoral goddess Hera. In this view, human beings are simply the toys of the gods who manipulate them for their sport. Human beings have no control over their own attitudes and actions, and therefore they have no responsibility for their deeds. This view robs any myth of its power and its ability to teach moral values. By enhancing the power of the gods, this interpretation demeans human beings.

In all Greek myths, an interplay occurs between the role of the gods and the role of human choice in human behavior. The power of these myths resides in the fact that the inherent nature of the human personality often prevents characters from practicing the principles of "know thyself" and "nothing in excess; everything in moderation."

Given Jason and Medea's respective personalities, the plot of *Jason and the Golden Fleece* would occur even if the Olympian gods do not exist. Eros's arrows represent the unpredictable and emotional (irrational) nature of sexual attraction. Jason and Medea reveal their own psychological motivations for the attitudes and actions for which Hera claims responsibility. Human success and failure can always be attributed to the individual in particular circumstances or to luck, rather than to the gods.

In Greek myth, the ways in which characters are punished for their attitudes and behavior can be attributed to the gods, or to gods who choose to act through human beings, or to the natural instinct of those who have been victimized to retaliate—independent of any god's wrath and assistance—with some form of retributive justice. It is important to realize that Jason does not suffer the consequences of his attitudes and behavior until he has compounded them in the following myth of *Medea.* Moreover, given the nature of Jason's personality, once Medea chooses to forsake her family and cast her lot with Jason, the consequences of her decision give birth to further consequences in the following myth.

35. **Contribution of the Olympian gods to reader response.** The gods serve many functions: (a) They place the characters in the myth in a moral universe, where mortals who behave unjustly, in time, will be punished. (b) They remain as ancient explanations for the psychological aspects of human behavior. (c) They enhance the story by making it a myth and, therefore, giving it a moral and didactic emphasis. (d) To the extent that the gods' human personalities make them less godlike, they enhance the stature of the human characters. Whereas the gods have nothing to lose, they never have to take any risks. In contrast, the human characters courageously persevere despite their knowledge of their own frailties and their own inevitable mortality.

36. **Role of prophecy in Jason's quest.** In the myths of many cultures, what is destined to occur, in fact, will occur—not because it is destined to occur, but because the inherent nature of the human personality causes it to occur. This is true of Greek myth in general, and it is true of *Jason and the Golden Fleece* in particular.

Zeus limits what Phineus may reveal. Therefore, Phineus avoids specific details. For example, he says that Aphrodite will offer help and that Jason should consider it. However, he does not explain the form that the goddess's help will take, and he does not tell Jason to accept it. Years later, Jason tells Medea that Aphrodite, rather than Medea, was responsible for the success of his quest since she and Eros made Medea fall in love with him. However, given Jason's personality, Medea's personality, and what Medea had to offer Jason, their relationship and its consequences are the result of psychology rather than divinity.

Moreover, the ability of heroes to act as if they are ignorant of known prophecies is both ironic and typical of human nature. Phineus lectures the Argonauts on the danger of the behavior pattern of *aretē* (excellence), *hubris* (excessive pride), *atē* (blind, rash behavior), and *nemesis* (retribution).

However, Jason is deaf to his words. Being certain that he will avoid this danger, Jason apparently views Phineus's words as the ramblings of an old man.

37. ***Aretē, hubris, atē,* and *nemesis* in daily life.** Newspapers, magazines, and television reveal how common a pattern this is in human behavior throughout the world. You may want to have your students bring in articles about the people who succumb to it. Examples include: (a) presidents of companies and leaders of countries who think that, because they are presidents or leaders, they can ignore the law and do what they wish to do; (b) media reporters who think that, because of their position, they can achieve fame by fabricating the stories they are reporting; (c) personal experiences of people who think that, given who they are, they can bend or ignore the rules.

38. **Heracles in Colchis.** If Heracles had arrived in Colchis with Jason and the Argonauts, Jason would have had no need for Medea. Given his personality, Jason would have been willing for Heracles to perform the tasks that Aeetes was demanding, and Heracles would have had no difficulty in performing them. Heracles also could have physically subdued the serpent that guarded the Golden Fleece and removed the fleece from the tree on which it hung. Therefore, it would have been in this way that Jason would have brought the Golden Fleece back to Greece. Moreover, once the Argonauts had returned to Iolcus, Heracles would have been strong enough to kill Pelias.

However, from the time of his birth, Hera hates Heracles because he is the child of her husband, Zeus, and a mortal woman. Therefore, Hera would never have permitted Heracles to gain the glory of performing Aeetes' tasks and capturing the Golden Fleece. Instead, she would have insisted that these honors go to Jason, who was her favorite. Moreover, Hera would have preferred that Medea murder Pelias for similar reasons. Therefore, it is consistent with Hera's attitude toward Heracles that, according to some myths, Heracles was forced to leave his heroic companions because Hera and Eurystheus would not permit him to take so much time off from his labors.

MEDEA (PAGE 204)

1. **Aeetes' monologue.** Aeetes' monologue reveals that he is a father, with a father's reactions to a trusted daughter's treachery. His monologue also reveals his intelligence and psychological insight as he seeks to cope with the surprise of Medea's treachery, to understand it, and to integrate it into what he had expected. Moreover, his monologue also reveals his capacity for rage and the fact that his heart and mercy are strangers.

Aeetes does not reveal his reasons for wanting to kill Medea himself. Possibly he has been so hurt and angered by the fact that it was Medea, a daughter whom he loved and trusted—rather than the sons of Phrixus, whom he distrusted—who behaved treacherously that he wants to be able to talk with her before killing her. Possibly he wants to listen to her side of the story, but possibly he only wants to direct his rage at her. Conceivably, but not likely, this meeting would change his mind about killing her.

Aeetes' monologue also functions as exposition in that it reveals the relevant events that have preceded the opening of this myth (related in detail in *Jason and the Golden Fleece*). Therefore, the reader learns about Helios's warning prophecy, the nature of Jason's character, the role of the sons of Phrixus and the goddess Hecate, the nature of Medea's gifts, and Medea's very human vulnerability. Moreover, Aeetes' questions about Medea's future with Jason foreshadow what will occur in this myth.

2. **Jason's reaction to Aeetes' fleet.** Consistent with his attitudes and behavior in the preceding myth, Jason's response to the Colchian fleet is pragmatic and prudent. He is certain that the Argonauts would lose a battle against the warriors of Colchis, and, therefore, he has no intention of initiating a fight. He would escape if he could, but he is certain that he cannot. Therefore, he responds in his typical way—by delegating to Medea whatever she can do better than he. It is no surprise that Jason tells Medea that it is up to her to save them.

What is new—although it is totally consistent with the nature of Jason's character—is that Jason would choose to save the Argonauts by returning Medea and her brother to their father. Now that he has acquired the Golden Fleece, he has achieved the glory that brings lasting fame, and, therefore, Medea is no longer useful to him. He feels no sense of gratitude or obligation toward her because of what she has done for him. He feels no obligation to keep his sacred promises to her. Moreover, he knows that Aeetes would kill Medea because of her treachery, but her fate at her father's hands does not concern him.

Although readers of the preceding myth may have doubted Jason's integrity, here he proves that he is incapable of loving anyone but himself and that his words to the contrary were a sham. What is important to Jason is that he remains alive, no matter what the moral issue and no matter what the heroic code. This attitude reveals Jason to be a totally self-serving, callous human being who will sacrifice his most solemn oaths and responsibilities in order to achieve a selfish goal.

3. **Medea's monologue.** Medea's monologue reveals her values. Whoever makes a sacred promise is obligated to keep it. A man of honor keeps his word. Medea has given up family and homeland for a stranger who appeared to be honorable. Now she realizes how mistaken she was in her evaluation of Jason, and therefore she calls upon the gods to curse him.

Medea's statement that she knew that she, alone, could save Jason reveals how her *aretē* (excellence) with herbs and drugs led to *hubris* (excessive pride) in her unusual skill. Her greatest strength led, through *hubris* (the thought that she alone could save Jason's life) to her greatest weakness, her *atē* (blind, reckless behavior) in which she helped Jason and so became a traitor to her family and country. Medea should have recognized that Jason's problem was not her responsibility—that, in fact, her responsibility was to her father. Her *nemesis* (retribution) is her loss of her family and her total dependence on a man who values her only to the extent that she can help him achieve his personal goals.

Other ways to save Jason existed. First, he could have retreated. Second, he and the Argonauts could have fought for the Golden Fleece. If Jason had died in this way, he would have died a noble death, and he would have preserved his honor. In the end, Jason survives, but without the honor and respect earned by traditional heroes.

Moreover, it is Medea herself, who, in presenting her dream to Chalciope, encourages Chalciope's involvement. Yet, it was Chalciope's responsibility to explain the issue of responsibility to her sons, and that would have been the best way to try to save their lives.

Medea's monologue extends back to *Jason and the Golden Fleece,* where she helped Jason, as well as forward into the future. Her evaluation of Zeus and Hera's reaction to Jason's scheming mind and cold heart foreshadows what eventually will happen to Jason.

4. **How Medea frightens Jason.** Medea's curse frightens Jason. He knows her power, having been the recipient of it. He knows that he would like to break his sacred oath. Therefore, he has ample reason to fear the wrath of the greatest of the Olympian gods.

5. **Medea's interior monologue.** Long, extended comparisons are known as *Homeric similes.* The Homeric simile that precedes Medea's interior monologue presents a situation that describes Medea's emotional response to her current situation. She is terrified, and she is grasping wildly for something that will save her.

Medea's thoughts then follow a pattern that is psychologically realistic. First, she criticizes herself for getting herself into this position. Second, she considers returning to her father, which she rejects. Third, she considers suicide, which she also rejects. Fourth, she realizes that she will do whatever is necessary to remain alive. Having come to this conclusion, she is psychologically prepared to murder her little brother.

6. **Jason and the murder of Apsyrtus.** Jason's ambition to return with the Golden Fleece and to remain alive would have motivated him to murder Apsyrtus. However, he probably would have been too afraid to do it against Medea's wishes. From her preparation for his tasks and her handling of the serpent, Jason knows the power of Medea's herbs and charms. Therefore, he would probably fear that she would use her skill with magic to preserve Apsyrtus's life and to harm his own.

Jason helps Medea with the murder because it is also in his best interest that Apsyrtus is killed. Moreover, Medea is more likely to perform this unspeakably immoral deed if he helps her.

7. **Medea's magic versus Apsyrtus's murder.** Medea's reputed ability to control rivers, the growth of flowers and grain, and the path of the moon reflects her ancient role as a Great Goddess, which includes her roles as Mother Goddess and Moon Goddess. This ancient identity appears again with regard to her rescue by Helios's chariot at the end of this myth. However, controlling weather is not one of Medea's abilities. She has godlike talent, but she is not

depicted as a goddess. Only Zeus, Hera, and Poseidon have the power to control the weather.

More significant is what Medea's willingness to murder her brother reveals about her love for Jason and its consequences. Until now, Medea has been a traitor to her father and her country, but she has not harmed anyone. With this deed, she reveals that she will do anything for Jason's benefit. Her love and devotion stand in sharp contrast to Jason's selfish and callous attitude toward her. Moreover, the consequences of the murder have a far-reaching effect on Medea's life. This murder cements Medea to Jason, no matter what the circumstances. Medea has entertained no hope of her father's forgiveness if she ever returned home. However, now, if she were ever to return home, she would be punished for the unspeakable crime of fratricide.

8. **Significance of Apsyrtus's sigh and hand.** Apsyrtus's sigh and hand are external symbols of Medea's internal psyche. She knows that she is performing an evil deed, and she feels as guilty as she should. As she says earlier, it is the first time she has acted so as to destroy life.

9. **Why the Argonauts do not stop the murder.** The Argonauts make no effort to stop the murder because it is in their own best interest that it occur. They may rationalize their abdication of responsibility by saying that Medea's brother is not their affair. However, evil deeds often occur because good people stand by and do nothing to prevent them. Their behavior is inexcusable. Zeus expects moral behavior from human beings. However, if Zeus did not exist, human beings still have the obligation—to themselves as well as to others—to construct a moral code and adhere to it.

10. **Alcinous's obligation and fear.** King Alcinous privately sympathizes with Medea and Jason, to whom he is also obligated since they are his guests. However, if Alcinous angers King Aeetes, the Colchian herald has declared that the warriors of Colchis will destroy Phaeacia.

Alcinous cleverly solves this conflict by confiding his decision—to protect Medea if she is Jason's wife—to Queen Arete before he plans to announce it on the following day. Then—either because Alcinous is asleep, or because Arete knows that he is pretending to be asleep—Arete feels free to convey her husband's decision secretly to Jason. In this way, Jason receives the opportunity to save Medea by marrying her.

Ironically, the Colchian threat turns out to have been empty. When King Alcinous appears before the Colchian commander accompanied by his armed warriors, instead of going to war, the Colchian commander defects. Rather than return to Colchis without Medea, he and his men remain on Phaeacia, where they become King Alcinous's allies.

11. **Why Jason marries Medea.** Jason marries Medea because, under these circumstances, he sees only advantages. Medea is beautiful, and she loves him. She has proved, with the murder of her brother, that she will do anything for him, and she is gifted in the use of herbs and magic. Equally important is the fact that Alcinous will protect their marriage, and therefore Jason does not

risk death from Aeetes or his warriors. Moreover, if Jason were to refuse to marry Medea, it would be embarrassing and, therefore, harmful to his reputation because Alcinous would have to return Medea to Aeetes, who would kill her.

12. **Hera's claim to having influenced Arete's thoughts.** Hera claims that she has given Arete the idea of revealing Alcinous's decision to Jason. Her timing reveals that she may be taking credit for Arete's independent response. Certainly Arete's response makes sense psychologically in terms of her personal interest in Medea. The debatable issue is whether human beings are free to choose, or whether the gods determine their behavior.

13. **Zeus's justice; Medea in Libya.** The Argonauts deserve Zeus's punishment because they made no attempt to stop Jason and Medea from murdering Apsyrtus. This makes them responsible for the crime, as well.

Medea does not help the Argonauts in Libya because she does not possess the skill to do so. Medea is godlike but not divine. Her abilities are limited to specific types of skills. Her divine ability to affect the growing season is an outworn appendage from her earlier role as the Great Goddess, with specific references to her aspects as Mother Goddess and Moon Goddess.

14. **Significance of why Medea kills Pelias.** One interpretation is based on the view that human beings are puppets or pawns of the gods. Therefore, Medea kills Pelias because Hera contrived to bring her back to Iolcus with Jason expressly for this purpose. This view deprives Medea of any ability to influence the course of her own life. Moreover, it reveals Hera to be callous and cruel since she does not care that she has forced Medea to forsake her father, her family, and her homeland in order to be available to murder Pelias for Jason.

The following interpretation is more complex: Once Jason determines to kill Pelias, Medea volunteers to kill him because Pelias gained the throne illegally, and he is responsible for the death of Jason's parents. Therefore, in a system in which retributive justice (an eye for an eye) is the rule, Jason is obligated to avenge his father's death by killing Pelias. For Medea to volunteer to be Jason's agent is perfectly consistent with her personality and her values. She has been willing to do anything to help the man she loves, and by killing Pelias herself, once again she is preserving Jason's life (see *Jason and the Golden Fleece*). Given what we know about Jason, he must know that Pelias is stronger and more clever than he is and, therefore, that he is no match for Pelias. Having murdered her brother, whom she loved, murdering a ruthless king would not bother Medea's conscience.

Medea's murder of Pelias reveals what a good friend and what a dangerous enemy she is. In *Jason and the Golden Fleece*, Medea used the same process to rejuvenate Jason. Here, she plays on Pelias and his daughters as a skilled musician plays on her instrument. Medea's performance reveals how insightful she is with regard to human nature and how creatively she accomplishes her goals. With Pelias, she appeals to his very human desire for rejuvenation. With Pelias's daughters, she appeals to their obligation to obey their father's wishes.

Jason's decision to permit Medea to murder Pelias is still another example of his pragmatic and prudent behavior. Once again, Jason is delegating to Medea something that she can do better than he. His decision is prudent because he knows that Medea's method of murdering Pelias will be more subtle than his own direct confrontation. Therefore, she will be able to murder Pelias with no risk to his (Jason's) life, with little risk to her own life, and with greater certainty of success.

However, Jason's behavior is also cowardly in that he hides safely behind Medea while she takes the risks and absorbs the guilt of a murder that is his own obligation. This is consistent with Jason's earlier pragmatic acceptance of Medea's help, his displays of cowardice in the course of performing the tasks that Aeetes demanded of him, and his prudence in permitting Medea to capture the Golden Fleece. It is important to note that no traditional hero would choose to behave as Jason does whenever he confronts the risk of losing his life.

Pelias's murder reveals how much Medea will do for the man she loves. Conversely, it reveals how much Medea might do to harm Jason should she realize that he does not love her.

15. **Why Pelias's daughters kill Pelias.** Hera does not choose Jason for this task because he could never murder Pelias without the support of a great group of warriors. However, Medea possesses the creative intelligence to contrive a successful plan. Yet Hera is not necessary in order for Pelias's death to occur in this way. Medea chooses to have Pelias's daughters kill their father because this method is more horrible in that it makes Pelias's daughters directly responsible for their father's death. This method is also safer for Medea in that it enables her to escape before Pelias's daughters discover that their father will never return to life.

16. **Hera's response to Pelias's death.** In the process of avenging her dishonor, Hera does not hesitate to have Medea—unknowingly—ruin her own life in order to carry out Hera's will. So it is that Medea becomes Hera's pawn. First, Hera asks Aphrodite to have Eros make Medea fall in love with Jason. Then Hera makes certain that, no matter what happens, Medea's thoughts lead her to return to Hellas with Jason.

Hera does not care about Medea's treachery and the murder of Apsyrtus. Hera does not care that she leaves Medea in a strange land where she cannot return to her country and, instead, must depend totally on Jason in order to survive and prosper. Once Medea achieves Hera's goal with regard to Pelias, Hera shows no obvious concern about Medea's welfare. Yet Hera will later take Medea's part against Jason, her old favorite. Hera is Protector of the Wedding-bond, and when Jason breaks that bond, he dishonors Hera as well as Medea. Therefore, the time comes when Hera also punishes Jason.

However, it is also possible to view Hera as a goddess who exists in name only—simply as a vestige of earlier religious belief and literature in which she was important—and to view human beings, through their attitudes and actions, as bringing their troubles on themselves. When they overstep the moral boundaries that should govern their lives, other human beings punish them for it. According to this view, Pelias dies because he illegally took his brother, Aeson's, kingdom and later caused Aeson's death. Therefore, Medea—who is related by marriage to Aeson's son (the person who is obligated to take revenge)—punishes Pelias.

17. **The universe in which Medea and Jason live.** Zeus's punishment of everyone aboard the *Argo* reveals a world ruled by a divinity who demands moral behavior from human beings. Those who behave otherwise are punished, either directly by the gods or indirectly by other human beings. This leads readers to expect that all immoral behavior will be punished. Therefore, Jason should be punished if he breaks his oath, and Medea should be punished for murdering her brother.

Hera joyfully responds to Pelias's death because it is her retribution for his having dishonored her. Her response reveals a moral universe. Gods expect human beings to respect them, and either directly or indirectly through human beings they punish those who ignore or dishonor them. Hera and Zeus, in particular, are known for their powerful forms of revenge.

18. **Creon's view of Jason.** Creon considers Jason to be the greatest hero of Hellas (in his time) because he went forth to the end of the known world, braved numerous dangers, performed impossible tasks, and returned with the prized Golden Fleece.

Not only is this Creon's point of view, it is Jason's point of view, as well. Acastus and Medea might have a different opinion because they know more about the nature of Jason's character. Creon accepts Jason even though he knows very little about him, and Jason does not let the nature of his character cast a blemish on his heroism.

This situation is true to life in that many heroes are not people whom one would choose as a friend. Often, people make heroes of others because of their accomplishments, without knowing—or without caring—about the means they chose to achieve their goals.

19. **Medea as an ideal wife.** Medea is an ideal wife, even according to Hellenic values, in that she is devoted to her husband and her children. Before Jason abandons her, she has done whatever he has needed her to do, no matter what the personal sacrifice.

However, before they reached Corinth, Jason revealed himself to be totally self-centered, arrogant, and ambitious. Therefore, despite these happy years, it is not surprising to see how Jason reacts once the opportunity presents itself, and it would not be surprising to learn that Medea still wishes that she had chosen to marry a better man.

However, even if it had been possible, even if the situation had presented itself, and even if Medea had wanted to leave Jason for another man, she would never have betrayed her marriage vows, because they are sacred. (Abandonment would not be an issue for Jason, as it is for Medea, because Jason is male and a Hellene. He would always find a place in a Hellenic community, and he would find another wife with whom he would have other children.)

Moreover, having murdered her brother and King Pelias, Medea must remain with Jason. When she cast her lot with him, she gave up family and homeland. Consequently, from that time forth, she has had no viable choices. She has condemned herself to have to help Jason in every way that she can so that he will not abandon her. Therefore, even if it were possible to leave Jason, even if Medea wanted to leave Jason for a better man, and even if she would betray her sacred marriage vows, a better man probably would refuse to consider her. Medea is a barbarian woman in a Hellenic country. Moreover, her deeds would frighten anyone but a man who is as ambitious as Jason, and Medea would not choose to marry another Jason.

20. **Jason's interior monologue.** Jason's interior monologue reveals how arrogant he is and that he is suffering from the behavior pattern of excellence (*aretē*), excessive pride (*hubris*), blind and reckless behavior (*atē*), and retribution (*nemesis*). His *aretē* is based on his successful leadership of the expedition to fetch the Golden Fleece. His success leads him to state that no human being is his equal, which is *hubris*. This *hubris* leads to his *atē* (blind, reckless behavior). Because Jason thinks he is the best of all men, he thinks that he is entitled to leave his wife and marry the daughter of a powerful and wealthy king.

   Jason's monologue foreshadows his retribution (*nemesis*), which is sure to follow from his abandonment of Medea. We already know how much Medea loves Jason, how much she has sacrificed for him, and how dangerous an enemy she is. Now Medea's boundless love will turn into a boundless hatred, and she will find a suitable way to punish him.

21. **Creon's conversation with Jason.** Like Jason, Creon is arrogant and self-serving. His *aretē* is his power as king of Corinth. He suffers from *hubris* in that his position and power lead him to think that he is omnipotent—that he can do and have whatever he wants, no matter what it is. Creon's attitudes reflect what he considers to be good for him, and he is certain that the gods agree with his perspective and his judgment. He believes that he will profit from having Jason as his son-in-law and, therefore, that this marriage will also be good for his daughter and good for the people of Corinth. Having established what is good for himself, Creon adopts attitudes and actions that support his point of view.

   For example, Creon absolves Jason of the murder of Pelias and puts the entire blame on Medea. Moreover, because she is a Colchian, Creon views Medea as a barbarian and, therefore, as an illegitimate wife. His arrogance and callousness toward women are revealed by his indifference to Medea's feelings, by the speed with which he is making her leave Corinth, and by the lack of legal support for women and resident aliens in Corinth under his rule. Creon is the law, and, therefore, when Creon considers resident alien females to be objects rather than human beings, they have no more rights than rocks or trees.

   Creon's *hubris* leads to *atē* in that his attitude toward Medea enables him to bless Jason's abandonment of his wife and to encourage Jason's marriage with his own daughter. Jason and Glauce's marriage, in turn, leads Creon to commit a further blind and reckless act—his banishment of Medea. Consequently, Creon's statements to Jason foreshadow his *nemesis* in the form of Medea's retribution.

22. **Significance of Creon's decision to banish Medea.** Once Creon approves Jason's marriage to Glauce, he must reckon with Medea as a spurned woman. Therefore, he must fear her revenge, and he must banish her in order to protect himself and his daughter. This is another aspect of his blind recklessness (*atē*) since he does not foresee the consequences (*nemesis*) of this act. Medea's banishment adds fuel to the fire of her revenge. However, Creon's decision does not provoke Medea's retribution. Jason's betrayal and abandonment are the primary cause; Glauce's acceptance and Creon's approval of that marriage are only secondary causes.

    The greater significance of Creon's decision is that it removes Medea's option to leave Corinth. Because Creon has commanded it, Medea cannot accept it without demeaning herself by subjecting herself to Creon's greater power. As a resident alien who no longer has a male to sponsor her and as a female, Medea has few acceptable ways to respond to her terrible situation. However, if Creon had not forced her to leave, she could have chosen, of her own free will, to take her children and leave Corinth. Exile would have been just as precarious and painful. However, Medea would have avoided the embarrassment and the mockery she so fears by taking the initiative herself. In this way, she could have exerted control over her own life and also punished Jason for his betrayal and abandonment.

23. **Medea's feminist interior monologue.** Medea's interior monologue reveals the position of women in the male-dominated society of ancient Greece, where the life of a married woman is difficult and the life of an unhappily married woman is disastrous. In Euripides' day, in Athens and, he assumes, in Corinth, once a woman marries, she is totally dependent on her husband. Moreover, she must accept her lot—whatever it is and even if it dishonors her—because to leave her husband is to break a sacred oath, and a woman needs a male protector.

    Meanwhile, from the male point of view, a women has an easy life. She should be docile in mind as well as in behavior, and, if she is wise, she will avoid resentment by making no attempt to be clever or outstanding in any way.

    These comments are thousands of years old, and yet many women experience these attitudes today. In fact, women in many parts of the world remain in the position that Medea describes.

24. **Medea's rage.** Medea is outraged that Jason has betrayed and abandoned her by disregarding his sacred oaths and marrying Glauce. King Aegeus of Athens will confirm Medea's point of view. Jason has dishonored Medea, and therefore he has dishonored himself. Moreover, Jason has dishonored the gods and shown disrespect to their power. Therefore, he should expect their judgment.

    However, Medea accompanies these accusations with the further accusation, "after all I have done for you." First, Medea enabled Jason to perform the tasks that her father demanded of him; she put the serpent guardian of the Golden Fleece to sleep; and she told Jason how to remove the fleece from its tree. These acts made her a traitor to her father and country and compelled her to cast her lot with Jason. Soon thereafter, she had no viable choice but to agree to murder her brother. Upon reaching Hellas, she willingly took upon herself Jason's obligation to murder King Pelias. Consequently, Medea has ruined her life for Jason in that she has condemned herself always to be a stranger in a strange land. In return, Jason owes the success of his quest and his stature as a Hellenic hero to her.

Now Medea knows that Jason was not worth her sacrifice. He has proved himself to be ambitious, self-serving, callous, and unprincipled. He has always been happy to have her do his dirty work. Now he is all too happy to move on to a younger woman who is the daughter of a powerful and wealthy king.

As a result, Medea is also filled with rage against herself. She realizes that she permitted her passion to rule her reason, and it led her to sever her ties with her family and homeland. She realizes that her passion for a beautiful face, a godlike form, and honey-sweet words led her to give her total love and devotion to a stranger who was only pretending to love her. She realizes that, in reality, she has cast her lot with a shallow and ambitious man whose real intention was to exploit her—to use her love for him as the way of achieving what he wanted. Therefore, Medea has done what it is often human nature to do. She has turned her rage against herself into additional rage against Jason.

Medea will destroy Glauce in order to destroy the person Jason values, thus leaving him without the woman he loves. She will destroy Creon for permitting Jason to marry Glauce and for banishing her from Corinth.

Medea will use deception because she does not possess the physical strength or political power to deal with Jason on his ground. She must use creative intelligence, cunning, and deception, the weapons of those who are weak and powerless. Often the weak and powerless turn the stereotypical ways in which their enemies view them into weapons that work on their own behalf. Medea does this when she deceives Jason by pretending that she is sorry for her hostile remarks and by pretending that she is celebrating Jason's second wedding by sending his new wife wedding gifts. This seems so logical to Jason that he never questions her honesty, her motives, or the nature of her gifts.

25. **Purpose of Medea's accusations.** Medea's accusations give Jason the opportunity to deal appropriately with her situation and his responsibility for having created it. She lays the issues on the table: Jason's abandonment and betrayal; his breaking of his sacred vows; her vulnerability in her exile; and her anger and remorse over her trust in him.

26. **Analysis of Jason's response.** Jason's response reveals his arrogance, both as a human being and as a Greek. He credits Aphrodite and Eros for his winning of the Golden Fleece because he assumes that Eros made Medea fall in love with him. Jason's attitude relegates Medea to being a puppet or pawn of the gods. Yet he is too impressed with himself to recognize that, if Medea is a

puppet or pawn, then he must be as well. Ironically, this attitude of Jason's demeans him, since it assumes that he was not appealing enough to motivate Medea's sympathetic response.

Jason conveniently forgets the role that he played in establishing their relationship. Medea did not initiate their relationship; he did. He needed Medea's particular skill with herbs—for which Aphrodite and Eros deserve no credit. Therefore, he set forth to win Medea's love and, with it, her help.

Jason's praise of the Hellenes and their superiority over other peoples reflects Athenian, and presumably Corinthian, belief in Hellenic cultural and political superiority. Euripides is using Jason to force his Athenian audience to take a close look at themselves. Given how Jason is behaving, not only Medea, but everyone would have to be deaf and blind not to realize that Jason—rather than Medea—is the barbarian. He is ignoring religious law even if the law of the state condones his behavior.

When Jason credits himself with making Medea famous, he is reflecting his own interest and value in such fame. In fact, Medea feared, rather than desired, the songs that the poets would sing about her treachery.

Jason has surely told Glauce that he loves her. However, when he tells Medea that he did not marry Glauce for love, he is consciously telling a lie, but he is probably telling the truth. Jason appears to be incapable of truly loving anyone except himself. His declaration that he married Glauce in order to obtain the social position and security to which he is entitled is true. That he feels so entitled to it that he would break his sacred marriage vows in order to obtain it reflects his *hubris* (excessive pride) and the blind and reckless nature of his behavior (*atē*). Jason's claim that he married Glauce so that Medea and their children would profit from it is a lie. Jason would have known that an illegitimate wife and her children can acquire no rights through his second marriage.

When Jason blames Medea for her fate, his accusation has no foundation. Given Medea's murder of Pelias, Creon would have feared and banished her even if Medea had remained docile and mute. Creon could not have afforded to trust her. The fact that Jason blames women for the trouble in the world reflects the extreme to which he is going in order to remove himself from any responsibility for the troubles that engulf Medea.

Finally, Jason's transformation of catastrophe into good fortune reflects what his attitude would be if he were in Medea's place. Jason always fears death. (Remember his attitude preceding Apsyrtus's murder. Also see *Jason and the Golden Fleece.*) Therefore, Jason truly believes that exile is far better than death. Jason has actually come to help Medea. He would do what he says he will do. After all, Medea is leaving, and he is looking forward to a fine new life. Now, and in this respect, he can afford to be generous and kind.

27. **Jason's request for his sons.** Jason's declaration of love for his sons and his request to keep them appears in Seneca's version of Euripides' *Medea,* rather than in Euripides.

Jason's request gives Medea the idea of how to punish him. Since his sons mean more to Jason than his life, Medea could murder them and so leave Jason bereft of what he loves best. However, this idea does not become a plan until after Aegeus appears. Aegeus will confirm the importance of sons to a man, and he will promise Medea refuge in Athens.

28. **Medea's refusal of help.** Despite what he says, Jason is not Medea's friend. Therefore, Medea will accept nothing from the person who is responsible for her situation. Medea feels that she cannot leave quietly because that would condone Jason's unjust and immoral behavior, and she would leave having tolerated the dishonor. She later reveals her belief that this solution would give her enemies reason to ridicule her and that the sound of their laughter would accompany her wherever she goes.

    Conversely, Medea feels that if she strikes back, she is making both a private and a public statement to the effect that she will not permit her husband to succeed in dishonoring her. Then, when she leaves, she has displayed courage and skill, and she has gained the respect of her enemies.

    The extent to which this is an error of judgment on Medea's part is debatable. Some people forgive and forget, whereas others do not. To Medea, honor means more than life. To Jason, life means more than honor.

29. **Medea's statements about Jason's future.** Medea's statements about Jason's future foreshadow what will happen to him because Greek myth instructs members of its culture about proper human behavior. In Greek myth—more often than in real life—the nature of a person's character determines what will become of her or him.

    Second, by the time of Homer's *Odyssey,* the Greek gods are perceived as dealing justly with human beings. Among themselves, they are usually portrayed as acting very much like human beings. Nevertheless, when it comes to intervening in human affairs, they listen to those who respect them and pray for their help, and they deal harshly with those who do not respect them. It is not surprising that those who disregard the presence of the gods and the moral principles they reinforce usually mistreat human beings as well. Therefore, they would be punished by other human beings if the gods did not punish them. Jason is an excellent example.

    Third, the Greek audiences who heard or watched a performance or reading of this myth already knew what happened to Jason and why. Of interest to them would be how a particular playwright or author relates the myth.

30. **Jason's response to Medea.** Given that he broke his sacred promises to Medea, Jason's statement that he has no fear of the gods because Zeus surely supports his behavior reveals *hubris* (excessive pride) and arrogance. Medea is correct when she declares that Jason knows very little about himself and equally little about the gods.

31. **Significance of Medea's curse.** Medea's curse chills the human soul because it describes a way of life that is worse than death. Jason, who prizes life above all, will have nothing but his life. Medea's curse foreshadows what will happen to Jason. Medea will restate this curse in the form of a prophecy at the

end of the myth. Given that Medea is rescued by Helius's chariot, it is clear that Zeus and Hera support her values and that they will honor her prayer.

32. **Aegeus's role.** Aegeus influences Medea's behavior by emphasizing the importance of children, particularly sons, to a male. Because Medea has borne Jason two sons, Aegeus's comments about his childless situation reinforce Medea's idea of depriving Jason of his sons, and she will now decide to murder them.

Moreover, Aegeus criticizes Creon and Glauce, as well as Jason, for their roles in creating Medea's situation. In his opinion, all three have behaved immorally by dishonoring Medea, and their behavior has invited the gods to judge them. Consequently, Aegeus's views support Medea in her desire to punish them.

Finally, by offering Medea sanctuary in Athens, Aegeus gives Medea an escape hatch in that she will now have a destination to which to flee.

Aegeus's role in terms of the audience and reader is equally important. Aegeus is an impartial outsider and, since he is the king of Athens, his opinion matters. His reactions to Jason's behavior and to Medea's situation reveal how Euripides' Athenian audience and today's readers should view them.

33. **Medea's gifts and apology to Jason.** Being a woman and, in addition, a resident alien, Medea's only power lies in deception. If she is to succeed with her plan, Glauce must receive and put on the poisoned garments that Medea will send her. Medea accomplishes these goals through words and deeds that reveal her insight into the nature of both Jason and Glauce. First, she apologizes to Jason so that he will permit their sons to deliver her gifts and so that he will accompany their sons in order to be certain that Glauce receives them. Medea knows that Jason is so arrogant, so certain of his innocence, and so convinced of his generosity that he will believe her change of heart with regard to their sons and her generosity with regard to her gifts. Second, Medea sends Glauce gifts that are so appealing that she knows that Glauce will rush to put them on with no fear of the person who sent them.

34. **Medea's vacillation about her children.** Society is responsible for Medea's situation in that it fosters an environment that condones Jason and Creon's attitudes and behavior. Only Creon could have prevented Jason's act, and Creon approves it because he expects that he and his family will profit from it. Creon is the law. Consequently, when Creon approves of Jason's betrayal and abandonment of Medea, Medea has no legal protection, defense, or remedy. She has only two choices: She can attempt to protect, defend, and remedy her situation herself, or she can accept her terrible situation and attempt to make the best of it.

It is not surprising that Medea resents her position. She is a resident alien who has no male to protect her, and she is a woman. Moreover, she is also the daughter of a great king and a priestess of the goddess Hecate. Certainly Medea is correct in her assumption that a moderate response to Jason's betrayal and abandonment will save the lives of her children, but it will do nothing to remedy her situation. She would be no more than a helpless victim: of Jason, of Creon, and of their society. Medea knows that she cannot hope to change Corinthian society. Therefore, given the choice between protecting, defending, and remedying her situation as best she can, or accepting and making the best of it, she chooses to assert herself by defying Jason and Creon.

Medea views herself as being in a no-win situation. She recognizes that she is punishing Jason by killing her innocent children, but she cannot tolerate the thought of condoning Jason's abuse and hearing her enemies laughingly mock her. However, as Medea says, "What mother can kill her children?" Medea must vacillate in order to be a sympathetic character. She must find this deed as repulsive as Euripides' audience and all later readers find it. Therefore, in order to murder her children, Medea must be driven by forces that are beyond her control.

35. **Medea's self-knowledge.** Medea recognizes that the Corinthians may murder her sons because they brought Glauce the poisoned gifts. Euripides' *Medea* mentions this possibility, and, as the introduction to this myth explains, the Corinthians do murder Medea's children in other versions of her myth.

However, Medea knows that it is not the threat of the Corinthians but her great rage that overpowers any thought of moderate, reasonable behavior. She is driven by forces that are beyond her control—Jason's betrayal and abandonment of her and her overwhelming rage over his behavior and her own blind and reckless behavior in casting her lot with him.

It is important that Medea knows herself because it makes her both a sympathetic and a tragic figure. Medea knows that she is the victim of her own passionate nature. She knows what she must do, why she must do it, and the consequences. She knows that the Greek principle of "nothing in excess; everything in moderation" is best, but her rage will be satisfied with nothing less than depriving Jason of the sons he loves. She knows that she is murdering innocent children and that she is depriving herself of their companionship and love. Yet she must go through with her plan regardless of the personal cost to her. Despite all of Medea's insight, her emotions are too powerful to be ruled by her reason, and despite all of her skill with herbs, she cannot help herself.

Medea's myth causes readers to pity Medea and fear for themselves. In Medea, they see the suffering that her uncontrolled passions bring her, and they fear their own vulnerability to the rule of such passion in their own lives.

36. **Description of Glauce and Creon's deaths.** The deaths of Glauce and Creon involve a sudden reversal of fortune that is far greater than what their callous actions deserve. This causes the audience and reader to pity them and to fear that such unexpected and undeserved catastrophe might occur in their own lives. Besides the fear of sudden death, the audience and reader realize that, like Creon and Glauce, they too might find it easy to overstep the boundaries that preserve the rights of others, and, therefore, suffer a sudden reversal of fortune as well.

Members of the audience and readers pity Creon and Glauce because they are rich and powerful, yet they possess human limitations. Creon encourages Jason to disregard his marriage to Medea, permits Jason to marry his daughter, and then condemns Medea to exile. Despite his wealth and power, he cannot save his daughter, and he dies trying to rescue her. Glauce disregards Jason's marriage to Medea. She can marry the man of her choice, but she chooses a man who is already married to someone else. In this way, they are guilty of overstepping the boundaries that preserve the rights of others. However, the consequences they bring on themselves are greater than their rash deeds deserve.

37. **Jason's character.** Jason reacts to Medea's murder of his children with arrogance, self-pity, and a total lack of responsibility. He views himself as a superior Hellene (a Hellenic hero) to whom Medea has proved that a barbarian is forever barbaric. His only mistake was in marrying her.

    Consistent with Jason's view of himself and Medea, he prays to Zeus to punish Medea for murdering his children and to pity him for all the loved ones he has lost. Jason's statements about his status as a hero reveal his arrogance.

    Yet, two other statements reveal that, at a barely conscious level, Jason knows that he must take some responsibility for Medea's actions. First, in asking Zeus to defend him against anyone who would seek to tarnish his name, he obviously fears that possibility—and if he were as innocent as he claims, he would have no reason to fear public opinion. Second, in stating that he has acted as any Hellene would have acted in his place, he is defending his behavior—and if his behavior had been beyond dispute, he would have no need to defend it.

    At this point in the myth of *Medea,* Jason's fear for his reputation and his rationalization of his behavior are already part of the price that he will have to pay for his actions. In Chapter 1 of *Jason and the Golden Fleece,* Jason tells Pelias, "(A reckless man's) eyes are blind to what will come to be. And so, he walks in the dark. And he bears a burden that weighs heavily on his mind and his heart." With these words, Jason reveals his knowledge of the behavior pattern that he has now blindly and recklessly adopted and his knowledge of the price that this pattern exacts from its victims.

38. **Medea's command.** Euripides includes Medea's command to the Corinthians in his *Medea,* and it is explained by other versions of the myths presented in the introduction. Equally interesting is the fact that it is Medea who commands it as if she is a powerful goddess.

    In Euripides' *Medea,* Medea tells Jason that he will live to regret the day he treated her as he has, and that he will die the miserable death of a coward when a piece of the Argo falls on his head. In this version, Medea's prophecy of Jason's future appears earlier in the form of a curse. Now, however (in this version as well as in Euripides' version), Medea's prophecy appears in the form of divine revelation. Other than gods such as Zeus and Apollo, and sea gods and goddesses, only seers (who have received their gift from Apollo, god of prophecy) and oracles (humans through whom Apollo usually speaks) possess knowledge of what is to come.

Medea's definition of human wisdom is put into the final words of the Chorus in Euripides' version. However, there being no Chorus in this version, her statement is consistent with the nature of her wisdom, and it is also consistent with her closing role as a divinity.

39. **Helios's chariot.** On one level, Helios sends his chariot to rescue Medea because she is his granddaughter, and, being the daughter of two immortal parents, Medea is also immortal. (Her father, Aeetes, is immortal because he is the son of Helios, god of the sun, and a sea goddess. Her mother is either a sea goddess or Hecate, an Underworld goddess.)

However, on a more important level, Helios rescues Medea because Zeus, Lord of Justice, and Hera, Protector of the Wedding-bond, view her cause of action against Jason as legitimate. Jason is a selfish, arrogant, and dishonorable man who is justly punished. Because of Helios's chariot, Medea is able to confront Jason in safety, and the chariot's arrival marks Medea's reversal of fortune from undeserved misfortune to the satisfaction of having achieved her goals. Medea's rescue and her godlike ability to reveal Jason's future prove that the divine world (represented by Helios's chariot) and the human world (represented by Aegeus, king of Athens) both support Medea, rather than Jason. The gods support her despite her murder of her children. Aegeus will support her because he will keep his sacred oath. However, from this time forth until the day of his death, Jason will have nothing but his life.

In contrast, it is possible to view the arrival of Helios's chariot as Jason sees it—as the symbol of the irrationality of the universe in which Jason and Medea (and all human beings) live. From Jason's point of view, divine justice and Medea's rescue are completely incompatible since an evil person is being rewarded. Therefore, her rescue reveals Jason's (as well as any other human being's) inability to understand the nature of life experience and to control his life.

40. **Medea's murder of her children.** Medea's murder of her children symbolizes the price she is willing to pay in order to avenge Jason's betrayal and abandonment. It validates what she considers to be most important: the necessity of keeping a sacred oath; the sanctity of the marriage-bond; and the need a woman has to be respected by her husband. Compared to these issues, being a loving mother is secondary to her.

Medea fears that, unless she severely punishes Jason, she appears to accept his treatment of her. Moreover, she feels that, unless she destroys the only people whom Jason loves more than his life, he will never understand the injustice of his betrayal and abandonment. Because these are Jason's children, Medea feels that she must kill them. Because these are also her own children, Medea becomes a tragic figure.

Medea's tragic stature causes the audience and reader to react with pity and fear: pity for Medea's inability to control her overwhelming rage toward Jason, and fear for their own vulnerability to passion's rule. Had Medea acted more reasonably toward Jason and more lovingly toward her children, she certainly would have been a nicer human being. However, she would not have left an indelible mark on the minds and hearts of audiences and readers throughout the ages. Her universal appeal resides in the depth of her outrage against injustice and the extent to which she is willing to rebel against it—a capacity that is marked by her murder of her children.

41. **Jason's denial that the gods exist.** Jason's denial of the gods appears at the end of Seneca's version of Euripides' *Medea,* rather than in Euripides' *Medea.* In Euripides' version, Jason's last words are addressed to Zeus (to look down and see what Medea has done to him) while Medea stands on the roof above him. In this myth, it is possible to view Jason's denial of the gods both as a reflection of Jason's point of view and as a reflection of an attitude that is consistent with the nature of his character throughout this myth.

Jason believes that he is a just man who is unjustly punished. He believes that Medea is solely to blame for her terrible deeds and that he has no responsibility for her crimes. Therefore, he expects that the gods will punish Medea. To Jason, the fact that Medea escapes reveals that the gods do not exist, since Medea's freedom and their existence cannot both be true. In reality, Jason's point of view reveals both how little he knows himself and how his arrogance prevents the suffering he is experiencing from teaching him what he needs to learn.

In contrast, it is possible to view Jason's denial of the gods as expressing the irrationality of the universe in which Jason and Medea (and all human beings) live. From Jason's point of view, divine justice and Medea's rescue are completely incompatible. Zeus, Lord of Justice, would never permit Medea to escape. Therefore, either Zeus exists but does not care enough about human life to demand justice on earth, or Zeus and the other Olympian gods do not exist at all. Either way, her rescue makes no sense and, therefore, reflects the inability of human beings to comprehend the nature of the universe.

42. **Reversals of fortune.** Medea's situation reverses from undeserved misfortune to the satisfaction of having achieved her goals, whereas Jason's situation reverses from happiness to misfortune that many readers will think he deserves.

Readers who view Medea as a villain would say that her reversal is ironic. First, she murders Glauce, and then she murders her own children. However, a dragon-drawn chariot suddenly appears and rescues her. These readers view this as a fault in Euripides' version of the myth because, in their opinion, Medea's rescue cannot be justified.

Actually, Medea's reversal of fortune is not ironic because the internal structure of the myth does not support the above interpretation. Medea's cause of action is upheld and the nature of Jason's character is criticized by an impartial observer, King Aegeus of Athens. Moreover, the arrival of Helios's chariot represents divine approval of Medea's point of view.

In contrast, Jason's reversal of fortune is ironic. Jason suffers from the behavior pattern of *aretē* (excellence), *hubris* (excessive pride), *atē* (blind, reckless behavior), and *nemesis* (retribution). The source of Jason's *aretē* is the fact that he led an expedition to fetch the Golden Fleece and returned with it to Hellas. He believes that this success entitles him to have whatever he wants, no matter what the cost to others, and that the Olympian gods will support his point of view (*hubris*). Therefore, he betrays his sacred marriage vows and marries Glauce (*atē*), never foreseeing the consequences of this deed. However, the Olympian gods condemn Jason's arrogant assumptions and behavior, and through Medea's revenge, they punish him (*nemesis*). Therefore, Jason loses everything that he values—in fact, everything but his life. Medea points out a further irony to Jason—namely, that, if he had loved his wife as much as he loves his children, he would not have brought this tragedy upon himself.

It is clear to Euripides' audience and to the later readers of this myth who are familiar with the values transmitted by Greek myths that Jason's arrogant ambition will lead to an inevitable and disastrous fall from prosperity. Nevertheless, as the audience and reader become aware of the slippery slope that Jason treads, they pity him and they fear for themselves because it is too easy to become a victim of *hubris*.

43. **Blame for Medea's troubles.** Jason is to blame for Medea's troubles in that his ambition drives him to betray and abandon Medea. He is a self-serving, callous, disloyal, dishonorable, and cruel human being. Society permits Jason to behave as he chooses, but it does not force him to mistreat Medea. Creon responds to Jason and encourages him because he and his daughter will profit from Jason's ambition. However, Jason must be held responsible for his own behavior. He did not have to take advantage of all that his society permits. He could have set moral standards for himself and lived by them. He could have honored his sacred oaths because he had made them. He could have remained loyal to his wife because he had married her. Because he is a male, and he is viewed as a great hero, Jason has the opportunity to make choices. His responsibility is to choose well.

Creon is to blame for Medea's troubles in that he permits Jason to marry his daughter, and then he banishes Medea from Corinth. Only Creon can prevent Jason's act, but Creon approves it because he expects that he and his family will profit from it. As Aegeus declares, Creon should have known better than to have permitted this marriage. However, Creon did not woo Jason for his daughter; he responds to Jason's initiative and his daughter's response to Jason. Creon's banishment of Medea adds flame to a pre-existing fire that would have continued to burn without this additional fuel. Creon is somewhat less responsible than Jason because he was not the initiator. However, he is equally ambitious and proud. Because he is the king of Corinth and the embodiment of Corinthian law, if he had been a more humane and sensitive human being, Creon could have made an effort to be more sympathetic to the position of the resident aliens and women in his kingdom.

Glauce is to blame for Medea's troubles in that she accepts Jason's courtship and proposal of marriage even though Jason is already a husband and father. However, Glauce did not pursue Jason; it was he who pursued her.

Medea has legitimate reasons to resent and hate Jason. However, no matter how Jason's attitudes and actions provoke her, she is not Jason's puppet. She is free to choose how she will respond. Medea is to blame in that, despite her insight into her own attitudes and feelings, she cannot stop her passion from ruling her reason, and therefore, she has no choice but to do whatever her passion demands. However, if Medea had let reason determine her behavior, her moderate response to Jason's betrayal and abandonment would have saved lives, including the lives of her children, but it would have done nothing to remedy her situation. She would have remained a victim: of Jason, of Creon, and of their society. Given the fact that Medea cannot hope to change society, her only reasonable choice is to accept a terrible situation and do her best to make the best of it. Given her passionate nature and the legitimacy of her cause, she refuses.

Hera is to blame for Medea's troubles in that she contrived to have Medea fall in love with Jason, help him acquire the Golden Fleece, and then return to Hellas with him so that Medea could be the means by which she punished Pelias for dishonoring her. However, once Medea has punished Pelias, Hera no longer brags about her manipulation of her. Moreover, Hera, as Protector of the Wedding-bond, sides with Zeus, Lord of Justice, and supports Medea in her accusations against Jason.

Society is responsible for Medea's troubles in that it fosters an environment that condones Jason and Creon's attitudes and behavior. However, Creon is the law, and, therefore, he leads Corinthian society. Consequently, when Creon approves of Jason's betrayal and abandonment of Medea, Corinthian society offers Medea no legal protection, defense, or remedy. Therefore, Corinth leaves Medea only two choices: She can attempt to protect, defend, and remedy the situation herself, or she can accept a terrible situation and attempt to make the best of it.

Responses will vary as to who is most responsible. However, Greek tragedy reflects the complexity of real life. No simple answers exist, but no-win situations do. Jason and Creon, as the leader of Corinthian society, should share Medea's responsibility. Jason is responsible for Medea's troubles, and Creon is responsible for her limited choices. The fact that Jason's society permits the mistreatment of resident aliens and women does not give Jason the moral right to betray and abandon her. The question is whether one can expect Creon to change the political, social, and economic nature of his society when the other Hellenic kings rule as he does. Certainly, no one can condone Medea's behavior, but it is possible to understand it.

44. **Sympathy for Medea and Jason.** Before Jason betrays and abandons Medea, she is the epitome of the kind, loving, respectful, understanding, giving, loyal, and supportive wife. In fact, in Medea, all of these qualities are excessive in that there is literally nothing that she has refused to do for Jason, including murder her brother. Earlier, she had sacrificed family and homeland when she treacherously enabled Jason to win and then capture the Golden Fleece. Yet readers can sympathize with the young Medea's passionate love for a heroic stranger and the ways in which one misstep leads to another.

After Jason's betrayal and abandonment, Medea still elicits the sympathy of the reader. Readers cannot help but empathize with a wife whose husband has rejected her in favor of a younger, prettier woman. They cannot help but empathize with the difficulties that Medea's banishment will bring her. Moreover, Medea's self-knowledge inspires a sympathetic response because all of her emotions—her rage as well as her love—are very human. Even Medea's guilt is very human because, as she is about to murder her children, she knows that she will never forget this deed, and that she will live the remainder of her life burdened by her love and loss.

However, although readers sympathize with Medea's tragic situation, most will find it impossible to sympathize with a woman who feels compelled to murder her children. Unfortunately, the qualities of being kind, loving, respectful, understanding, giving, loyal, and supportive that Medea has given so freely and generously to her husband evaporate with his betrayal and abandonment. Because they no longer exist within her, she cannot give them to her children. Jason's betrayal and abandonment transform these qualities into an equally excessive rage (composed, as it is, of a combination of rage against Jason and rage against her own blindness in choosing to cast her lot with him), and rage smothers all qualities that elicit sympathy.

Medea's inability to control her passions evokes fear as well as pity. Insightful readers can identify with Medea's all too human vulnerability, and the possibility that they, too, can be ruled by passion terrifies them. However, for other readers, the possibility is so terrifying that they resort to denial, and they reassure themselves that this could not happen to them.

In contrast, Jason is never truly kind, loving, respectful, understanding, giving, loyal, or supportive. Even when he is the heroic stranger in Colchis (in the preceding myth, *Jason and the Golden Fleece*), Jason never sacrifices anything for Medea. He speaks honeyed words with a golden tongue, but his words are deceptive in that they are his way of achieving his ambitious and self-serving goals. Earlier he wants to be able to perform the tasks that Aeetes demands of him and to acquire the Golden Fleece. Later, in the myth of *Medea,* he wants to improve his social status, political power, and economic prosperity. Therefore, in Jason, genuinely admirable emotions are always fleeting, at best, and it may be difficult to find readers who will sympathize with him.

However, although Jason deserves his misfortune, most readers would choose to have Glauce, Creon, and the children of Medea and Jason remain alive. It is punishment enough for Jason to be condemned to wander, alone and friendless, until his death. Unfortunately, however, this punishment could not be achieved without the deaths of Glauce and Creon, who would have prevented it.

45. **Medea's victory and defeat.** Medea is victorious in that she upholds her integrity as a good wife (before her betrayal and abandonment), she retains control over her own life, and she escapes unharmed from Corinth. Moreover, she succeeds in punishing Jason by destroying everything he values.

However, Medea defeats herself in that—as necessary as her actions may be in order to assert herself, protest her betrayal and abandonment, and punish Jason—the price she pays is exorbitant. She loses her children. Moreover, from that time forth, she must depend on the kindness of friends and strangers.

Medea is a heroine in that she refuses to be victimized by her husband and his society. Despite the personal cost, she refuses to act in a way that will betray her values: love, honor, respect, and loyalty. She sees the Hellenic prejudice against wives, women, and foreigners, and she condemns it. She insists on being respected as a wife, as a woman, and even as a foreigner. She is not only a woman of words, she is a woman who supports her words with deeds. She courageously rebels by using the only weapons that a woman in a male-dominated society possesses: creative intelligence, cunning, and deception. She skillfully punishes Jason by destroying all that he values. First, she kills Glauce—Jason's source of social status, political power, and wealth—by sending her secretly destructive gifts that appeal to her vanity. Then she kills the only people Jason loves more than himself, his sons.

Medea is a villain in that the violence of her acts is directed at Jason, and yet it destroys the lives of people who are either not as guilty (Creon and Glauce) or who are totally innocent (her children).

46. **Jason as a tragic hero.** Arguably, Jason can be described as a basically good man—especially during his youth and the period described in the preceding myth, *Jason and the Golden Fleece*. He is an appropriate leader of the Argonauts because he is a good manager (his *aretē*). Being a man of words rather than deeds, he acts in a conciliatory manner wherever possible and, therefore, seldom risks the lives of his companions. Moreover, in the myth of *Medea*, King Creon chooses him to be his daughter's husband, and King Aegeus is surprised to hear of his dishonorable behavior.

Jason is certainly not perfect, and his imperfections are psychologically consistent from the period of his young adulthood (in the myth of *Jason and the Golden Fleece*) and through the period of his maturity (in the myth of *Medea*). In *Jason and the Golden Fleece*, Jason's arrogance and driving ambition (his *hubris*) lead him to accept any means that will accomplish his goals. Therefore, he is willing to have Medea use her magic in order to assure him of success, even though this is cheating, and he is asking her to be a traitor to her father and her country. In the myth of *Medea*, Jason's arrogance and driving ambition (again, *hubris*) lead him to betray his sacred marriage vows, to forget all that he owes Medea, and to abandon Medea and to leave her an unsupported resident alien in Corinth—all in order to marry the king's daughter and thereby improve his social and political status and his economic prosperity.

Jason is blind in that he never anticipates the terrible consequences of his rash act (his *atē*). They involve Medea's murder of the princess and her murder of Jason's two sons (his *nemesis*). These are acts of a destructive and painful nature. Therefore, they cause Jason to experience a sudden and unexpected reversal from happiness to misfortune and to experience great anguish.

However, two aspects of Aristotle's description of the tragic hero are missing from Jason's situation. First is the question of whether Jason's misfortune is undeserved. Many readers will think that Jason's arrogance and excessive ambition bring him just what he deserves. His consistently arrogant and selfish attitudes and behavior make it difficult for most readers to pity him.

Equally important is the fact that, at last, through their suffering, tragic heroes gain self-knowledge and discover the relationship between their earlier rash act and the consequences that have brought their misfortune upon them. In contrast, at the end of the *Medea* myth, Jason's suffering has taught him nothing about himself. He sees no connection between his attitudes and behavior and his reversal of fortune. He feels no remorse because he casts all the blame on Medea. He does not even consider the possibility of taking some responsibility for what has happened to him. Medea's escape simply proves to him that the gods (and, therefore, divine justice) do not exist.

Jason is neither a sympathetic nor a tragic figure. He does not know himself, and so he is incapable of changing his behavior. His words and deeds are compelled by his boundless ambition and his excessive pride (*hubris*). Therefore, he acts with blind recklessness (*atē*). It never occurs to him that his behavior is immoral and, therefore, improper, and so he can see no reason why Medea and the gods might punish him for it (*nemesis*). His great arrogance prevents him from seeing the error of his ways. Therefore, from beginning to end, Jason remains self-serving, unprincipled, and unappreciative.

47. **The myth of *Medea* as a moral tale.** Medea's myth is clearly a moral tale in that it upholds love, honor, integrity, the viability of sacred oaths, and loyalty. These values are revealed twice: first, by an impartial Hellenic outsider when King Aegeus of Athens condemns Jason's betrayal and abandonment of Medea, and, at the end, by the Olympian gods when Helios's chariot rescues Medea, and she—now as a goddess—reveals that, from this time forth until the day of his death, Jason will have nothing but his life.

Moreover, the myth reveals how easy it is for a human being to be ruled by passion (love, hatred, rage, or unbridled ambition), rather than by reason, and the terrible consequences that follow when passion dominates human behavior. The myth emphasizes the dangers of ambition, fame, prosperity, and pride because, in excess, they become forms of *hubris* that lead to *atē* (blind, reckless behavior) and to *nemesis* (retribution).

Medea is ruled first by uncontrollable love for Jason. This leads her to become a traitor to her father and her country. Thereafter, she is a woman without a country. She must murder her brother in order to save her life. Moreover, having condemned herself to be totally dependent on Jason's protection, she feels compelled to do whatever will please him, including the murder of King Pelias.

Once Jason betrays and abandons her, given what she has sacrificed for him, Medea is ruled by uncontrollable hatred and rage. She feels that she must avenge his treatment of her by removing whatever he loves. When he loves their children, she is compelled to kill them. Leaving Jason bereft of all that he values is more important than preserving the lives of their children and improving the quality of her own life. In this way, Medea's passions compel her to bring extraordinary suffering upon herself.

The nature of Jason's character, as well as the nature of Medea's love for Jason, reveals that too much of a good thing is dangerous and brings suffering upon oneself and others. Jason's overwhelming passion is his unlimited ambition. He seeks continually to improve his situation, and he will use any means that will achieve this end. Jason's ambition is so consuming that Jason can only love himself.

In contrast to Medea and Jason's behavior, human beings should strive for self-knowledge and rational, moderate behavior that is characterized by self-control and self-restraint. Human beings should enjoy excellence (*aretē*), but resist feelings of excessive pride (*hubris*) because it leads to blind and therefore reckless behavior (*atē*), which, in turn, brings forth the dire consequences of retribution (*nemesis*).

48. **Significance of the gods in the lives of Medea and Jason.** The role of the gods in the lives of Jason and Medea reflects the attitudes and goals of the three ancient writers who are best known for their versions of these myths. First, Euripides, in his *Medea*, tells the story of Jason and Medea in Corinth. Although Jason and Medea appeal to Zeus and other gods, these gods do not influence the action until the end of the play.

Apollonius, who tells the story from the beginning until Jason finally returns to Iolcus (the myth of *Jason and the Golden Fleece*), wants to remind his readers of *The Iliad* and *The Odyssey* of Homer. Consequently, Hera, Zeus, and other divinities periodically influence the action in the this part of the myth. However, Zeus disappears once Boreas blows the *Argo* toward Libya, and Hera disappears once Medea has avenged Pelias's insult to Hera's honor.

Finally, Seneca, who adapts Euripides' *Medea,* is more sympathetic toward Jason and closes his tragedy with Jason's statement that "there are no gods."

Consequently, in *World Mythology,* the role of the Olympian gods in *Jason and the Golden Fleece* and in *Medea* reflects their various roles in these primary sources. However, even where the gods appear to take an active role in the lives of Jason and Medea, the question of whether Jason and Medea have control over their own lives or whether they are puppets and pawns of the gods is always debatable.

Until Jason and Medea take refuge in Corinth, it is possible to view them as the helpless victims of the amoral goddess Hera. In this view, human beings are simply puppets or pawns—the toys of the Olympian gods who manipulate them for their sport. Jason and Medea have no control over their own attitudes and actions, and therefore, they have no responsibility for their deeds.

However, given the nature of Jason and Medea's respective personalities and the history of their relationship (frequently alluded to in *Medea,* but revealed in *Jason and the Golden Fleece*), the plot of *Medea*—until Medea's rescue by Helios's chariot—would unfold as it does, even without the Olympian gods. After all, human success and failure can always be attributed to the individual's courage, strength, and skill in particular circumstances or to luck, rather than to the gods.

Later, in Corinth, Medea and Jason pray to the great Olympians, but Hera and Zeus remain invisible and silent. Consequently, it is possible for readers to agree with Jason's concluding statement that the gods do not exist, and, therefore, they play no role in human life. They do not manipulate human attitudes and behavior, and they do not reward those who are good and punish those who are evil.

However, it is important to realize that Jason's view of the gods is psychological rather than philosophical or religious. Like all of Jason's other views, this view is self-serving in that it conveniently denies that Jason deserves his reversal of fortune and his devastating retribution.

Moreover, if the reader is to make any sense of Medea's rescue and of the divine aspect of her proclamations, Zeus and Hera do exist in Medea's myth. As the Lord of Justice and Protector of the Wedding-bond, respectively, they validate Medea's accusations against Jason, and they support her revenge, bloody as it is. In Greek myth, it can be no other way. Without the Lord of Olympus, his siblings, and his immortal children, evil would not be punished, and the audience would have little to pity and nothing to fear.

If human beings were no more than puppets and pawns of capricious Olympian gods or if these gods did not exist, then Greek myths would not have their power, and they would not teach moral values. A myth that enhances the power of the gods demeans human beings. A myth that removes the power of the gods describes an irrational universe where the only justice is that which human beings establish and practice. Neither view represents the essence of Greek myth, where an interplay occurs between the role of the gods and the role of human choice in human behavior. The power of these myths resides in the fact that the inherent nature of the human personality often prevents characters from practicing the principles of "know thyself" and "nothing in excess; everything in moderation." Whenever this occurs, the offending characters bring their troubles upon themselves.

49. **Five examples of Homeric similes.** (1) the young shepherd who chases a stray lamb and finds himself tumbling down the mountain-side: a pastoral image from country life at the time that conveys Medea's terror as she faces her imminent death at the hands of her father's warriors; (2) the young widow who tearfully spins in the darkness: a pastoral image from life on a farm that conveys Medea's sorrow as she thinks of her future if Queen Arete refuses to help her; (3) the melting winter snow that becomes a raging and destructive torrent: a pastoral image from life in a mountain valley that conveys Medea's rage at the sight of the man who has betrayed and abandoned her; (4) the wolf outside the sheepfold that searches for a way to carry off a sheep: a pastoral image from life on a farm that conveys Medea's search for a way to avenge Jason's betrayal and abandonment; (5) a repeat of (3)'s simile that conveys Medea's rage toward Jason as she sends Glauce the wedding

gifts; (6) a repeat of (3)'s simile that conveys how Medea's rage pushes aside her reason and restraint; (7) the bees that the shepherd has smoked from their hive: a pastoral image of life in the country that conveys Glauce's torment from Medea's poisoned gifts.

50. **Relationship between *Jason and the Golden Fleece* and *Medea*.** The attitudes and behavior of the younger Medea and Jason predict the attitudes and behavior of their older selves. Medea the maiden falls in love with Jason the hero, and her youth and innocence make her vulnerable to the godlike face and form, and the golden tongue, of the sophisticated stranger from Hellas. Medea the maiden consciously permits her passion for this stranger to transform her from a loyal daughter into a traitor to her father and her people.

Years later, when Jason the husband betrays and abandons Medea the wife, once again Medea consciously permits her passion—this time, hatred and rage, to transform her from an appropriately modest wife into the murderer of their children and her husband's new wife. Part of her passion reflects her rage at her younger self for having permitted her to become Jason's pawn. However, Medea is inherently a passionate creature. Although she always possesses self-knowledge, she consistently rejects the rule of reason and chooses, instead, to let her passion determine her behavior.

Jason the hero is ruled by unbridled ambition, and he uses Medea in order to succeed in his quest for the Golden Fleece. First, he has no qualms about using sweet words in order to persuade Medea to become a traitor to her father and her country. Next, he has no qualms about cheating in order to perform the tasks that Medea's father is demanding of him. Then, he has no qualms about permitting Medea to lull the serpent to sleep so that he can collect the fleece. During their escape, he has no qualms about putting Medea into the position where either she or her brother must die, and once they return to Hellas, he has no qualms about letting Medea, on his behalf, contrive the death of King Pelias.

With this history, it is no surprise that the older Jason is still ruled by unbridled ambition. Therefore, it is no surprise that Jason has no qualms about betraying and abandoning his older wife for a younger, more beautiful, and wealthier woman who will enable him to become the next king of Corinth. Moreover, it is no surprise that the youth who consistently saw nothing immoral in his series of immoral acts should, as an adult, see nothing immoral in his rejection of his wife. It is no surprise that the youth who ignored the Colchian maiden's sacrifices on his behalf should, as an adult, place no value on all that his wife has done for him.

Consequently, knowing the younger Medea makes it much easier to understand and sympathize with the older Medea. Conversely, knowing the younger Jason makes it much easier to understand and dislike the older Jason. The older characters in the myth of *Medea* gain more emotional depth from the reader's knowledge of their younger selves in *Jason and the Golden Fleece*.

PYRAMUS AND THISBE (PAGE 247)

1. **Parents and children.** The typical "generation gap" exists in this story. Pyramus and Thisbe's fathers do not trust their children's judgment. They probably think that their children are too young to make the decision they have made and that they themselves, being older and wiser, know what is best for their children.

    Like many parents through the ages and throughout the world, Pyramus and Thisbe's parents try to force their children to obey their wishes. Like many children in the real world, Pyramus and Thisbe revolt, and their revolt creates a tragic situation both for themselves and for their parents.

2. **Attitude of fathers toward marriage.** Pyramus jumps to conclusions too quickly and with insufficient evidence, given that Thisbe's body is not present. He sees no signs of her being dragged away by the lion; he concludes that she is dead based solely on her torn and bloody cloak. Consequently, Pyramus acts rashly or imprudently, and his behavior is too emotional and too immature for the ideal husband. Marriage demands patience and more thoughtful responses. Both Pyramus's father and Thisbe's father may have recognized this weakness in Pyramus because they were in a position to observe Pyramus's behavior in many other situations.

3. **Why fathers are to blame.** When this story was written, marriages were arranged by the fathers of the couple, and the ability of a husband to support his wife was of paramount importance. Mothers may have been consulted; even the children involved may have been consulted. However, the extent to which other members of the family would have had a voice in the marriage agreement would have been determined by the particular personalities involved.

4. **Universal flaws.** Pyramus and Thisbe represent the flaw of emotional thinking. Pyramus concludes that Thisbe is dead too quickly and with insufficient evidence. He then kills himself immediately, without giving the situation time to correct itself and his bereavement, assuming that Thisbe had in fact died, time to heal. Thisbe kills herself immediately, without permitting the pain of her own loss to heal. For both Pyramus and Thisbe, the need to prove that they love each other equally by being willing to make the same sacrifices for each other is simplistic and therefore childish. They have a very romantic view of death.

5. **Aristotle's tragic hero.** Pyramus brings his misfortune—his death—upon himself by concluding too quickly, based upon insufficient evidence, that Thisbe is dead. Thisbe brings her misfortune—her death—upon herself because she has a very romantic view of death. Yet the question remains as to whether Pyramus and Thisbe are tragic figures. The fact that their behavior is so juvenile both enhances and detracts from their tragedy.

6. **Reaction of pity and fear.** Students who are close to the age of Pyramus and Thisbe (who might have been in their early teens) may empathize with them

and therefore pity them. Other students may find the behavior of Pyramus and Thisbe to be too juvenile and foolish to pity them.

It is not unusual for people to act based upon their emotional reactions to a particular situation. Therefore, students may fear that they, too, are vulnerable to Pyramus and Thisbe's flaws. They may have emotional reactions to a situation, which in turn will lead to self-destructive behavior.

Many people believe in an all-controlling Fate, which acts upon human life despite a person's best efforts to control his or her own actions. Given the chain of events in this story, with each situation leading one that is worse, the role of Fate in one's life can be a source of fear.

7. **Tragic aspects.** The tragedy in this story depends on the interplay of character and situation. Thisbe would not have committed suicide if Pyramus had remained alive. Pyramus would not have committed suicide if Thisbe had not dropped her cloak, and if the lion had not attacked it. On the other hand, it is because of his personality that Pyramus acts too hastily and with insufficient evidence. Moreover, it is because of her personality that Thisbe determines to make a sacrifice that equals the one made by Pyramus.

8. **Fate vs. bad luck.** Fate determines the arrival of the lion. Thisbe's personality determines that she runs from the lion and that she kills herself once she discovers that Pyramus has killed himself because he thought her dead. Pyramus's personality determines his reaction to his finding Thisbe's torn and bloody cloak. The role of the characters' personalities in this story make the tale more than one of bad luck, and they minimize the role of Fate in the story.

9. **Obedience to parents.** It is clear that if Pyramus and Thisbe had obeyed their parents, they would not have lost their lives. However, Ovid focuses on their love for each other, rather than on their foolishness or their disobedience. He tells the story from their point of view, and he does step in and criticize them.

10. **Mulberry tree.** The transformation of the mulberries from white to red highlights the tragedy in the story. The tree becomes the symbolic representation of the dead lovers. Because it is part of nature, the fact that the tree is sympathetic to the lovers and responds to Thisbe's wishes gives the love story greater depth and resonance. The tree, in the sense that it symbolizes the natural world, represents the universe and depicts it as being sympathetic to the plight and the tragedy of the lovers.

11. **The greater character: Pyramus or Thisbe.** Some students may consider Thisbe to be the greater character because she responds to a real death rather than an imagined death. Consequently, they may interpret her actions as being more thoughtful, and therefore more mature, than those of Pyramus. They may feel that Thisbe acts with greater courage than Pyramus does.

Other students may think that the two characters are too much alike. Pyramus takes the lead, and Thisbe follows that lead, no matter how foolish it is to do so.

12. **Enduring qualities.** This story contains the following appealing qualities: passionate love between two handsome young people; unsympathetic parents, who therefore are appealing to many of those who are young or young in heart; an unfortunate chain of events, each of which is dependent on the preceding event; plot and character that are so simply drawn that another writer can improve the story by adding greater characterization and a more complex plot.

THE AENEID (PAGE 255)

1. **Deaths of Aeneas's wife, Anchises, and Dido.** Virgil has the problem of taking a Trojan who has a known family and making him establish a home in a new country, where he must unite with the local people in order to establish a new nation. Consequently, all of Aeneas's emotional ties to the past must die, leaving him free to begin a new life in Italy. Students' opinions about the effect of this may vary. Some may feel that it makes the story seem contrived.

2. **How Aeneas changes.** As the story progresses, Aeneas becomes less human (and humane) and more like a puppet of the gods. He loses his freedom of choice and his flexibility, and he does whatever he must do in order to fulfill his destiny, no matter what the personal cost and no matter what the cost to other human beings. His departure from Dido marks the turning point, although his disregard for his wife in the rush from Troy is unusually callous for a loving husband.

3. **Aeneas and Dido as leaders.** Aeneas is a more effective leader because he does not let his emotions affect his judgment. Dido ignores the city she is building once she falls in love with Aeneas. Aeneas would never let anything keep him from his goal, and if his goal were to build a great city, he would do that no matter what the circumstances.

4. **Why Aeneas leaves Dido.** Students' opinions may vary. Possibly Aeneas is afraid to stand up to the gods. Aeneas's destiny is a great one: great political power and everlasting fame. It is hard to fault him for being unable to resist such a temptation, but it is also hard to like him for it. He is an ambitious human being, and Dido suffers because of his ambition more than Aeneas does.

5. **Justification for Aeneas's leaving.** Students' opinions may vary. One must consider the values that a person holds dear. Which is more important: love or fame? Aeneas would have had political power in Carthage, because Dido would have shared her kingdom with him. However, Aeneas could not resist the fame that he and his descendants would have if he established a community in Italy.

6. **Dido's love for Aeneas.** Dido's love for Aeneas affects her life in many ways: in return for short-lived friendship and love, she loses interest in her kingdom

and neglects her goals as queen. She stops supervising all work, bringing construction and even military training to a halt. Her love affair causes a scandal that is broadcast far and wide, making her people and those in neighboring communities lose respect for her. It makes her nation vulnerable to attack from the outside. She tells Aeneas that because of him she has lost honor and fame and has created a climate of political instability. When he persists in leaving her, she commits suicide.

7. **Character of Dido.** Students' opinions may vary. Dido serves as a foil for Aeneas. Her emotion and passion contrast with his cold intellect and iron will. She is willing to give up everything for him; he will give up nothing for her.

8. **Dido's suicide.** Dido commits suicide because she has so dishonored her name. She cannot live without shame and she refuses to live with it. She could have followed Aeneas, but no one would have respected a queen who ran after her lover, and Aeneas would have rejected her for the same reason that he left her—she was not part of his destiny. She could have married a neighboring king, but that would have been a political marriage, an arrangement Dido had never considered. She would not accept marriage without love.

9. **Appeal of Dido.** In making herself so vulnerable because of love, Dido wins the sympathy of the reader. Many students may take her part and criticize Aeneas.

10. **Death of Turnus.** The decision of whether or not Aeneas should have killed Turnus is a difficult one, both for Aeneas and for those who evaluate his predicament. On the one hand, a warrior does not kill a warrior who has surrendered. Such behavior is cruel, and only Achilles, after the death of Patroclus, is that inhumane.

   On the other hand, Aeneas was very fond of Pallas and owed some form of retribution for his death at the hands of Turnus. It was a typical incident of war, but Pallas was very young and was clearly outmatched by Turnus. The issue was a close one, and Aeneas clearly would have spared Turnus if the warrior had not been wearing Pallas's swordbelt as a badge of his victory. Yet wearing such badges was the custom of the time: for example, Hector takes Achilles' armor off Patroclus's corpse and wears it. In his depiction of the death of Turnus, Virgil shows that war can make beasts of human beings.

11. **Aeneas versus Turnus.** Students' opinions may vary. Turnus is defending his country against Aeneas, the invader. His treatment of Pallas is not beyond the ordinary cruelty of warfare. He kills him, but he returns his corpse to Evander. He is a victim of Aeneas's destiny.

12. **Role of prophecies.** Virgil wrote *The Aeneid* to glorify the reign of Augustus and Rome. Consequently, while on one level he uses the prophecies of Aeneas's destiny to activate Aeneas's ambition, on another level, these prophecies all advertise the glory of Augustus and the grandeur of Rome.

13. **Aeneas's sacrifices.** Aeneas sacrifices love in order to found Rome—first his wife (because he is too busy escaping with the household gods of Troy to think about her) and then Dido. His marriage to Lavinia is political, although, in time, he may love her. He also sacrifices his power to determine the course of his own life when he chooses to do whatever the gods tell him to do. That decision makes him a puppet or pawn. It causes him to hurt Dido, whom he loves. It causes him to war against a people who have done him no harm. Virgil wants the reader to question whether Aeneas's achievement is worth the sacrifice. How students feel about it will depend upon whether they sympathize with Aeneas's values.

14. **Character of Aeneas.** Aeneas is an ambitious person, and in this way he is most like the Greek hero Jason. When he must choose between Dido and Italy, he chooses Italy. When he must choose between peace in one land and war in Italy, he chooses war in Italy. When he must choose between saving Turnus's life or killing him, he chooses to kill him (politically safer than having to worry about a living enemy). The temptations he resists are those that would make him human: love and pity. The temptations he cannot resist are those connected with making his destiny a reality. He is less of a hero because of the choices he makes.

Supplementary Suggestions

1. A comparison of *The Aeneid* with *The Iliad* is natural, since Virgil patterned *The Aeneid* after Homer's epics.

2. Compare Aeneas, including his treatment of Pallas and Turnus, with Achilles and his treatment of Patroclus and Hector.

3. Compare Turnus and Hector.

THE FAR EAST AND THE PACIFIC ISLANDS

THE CREATION, DEATH, AND REBIRTH OF THE UNIVERSE (PAGE 291)

1. **Cycles.** The world of nature is a continuously repetitive series of cycles: spring, summer, autumn, winter; birth, youth, maturity, death, rebirth. People's lives follow this pattern from birth to death. The interpretation of rebirth varies from one culture to another.

2. **Views of life.** Students' opinions may vary. Technology improves, but other aspects of life may remain more or less the same within a particular culture as long as the values of that culture do not change. The concept of deterioration is probably the least appealing.

3. **Dharma.** The advantage of living according to the principle of dharma (the idea that each person has a particular code of righteous behavior to follow, depending upon his or her position in society) is that each person knows how he or she is supposed to behave in any situation. The disadvantage is a loss of flexibility and individuality. Individuals are evaluated based on the extent to which they follow a predetermined code of behavior.

    The concept of dharma may be used either to support or to oppose an effort to correct social injustice, depending on how it is interpreted. If those who are in positions of power, such as political leaders and employers, believe that dharma includes an obligation to work toward improving the living and working conditions of the people for whom they are responsible, then this concept will support an effort to correct social injustice. However, the concept of dharma may also be used to oppose an effort to change the status quo, even if the status quo involves what to a Westerner appears to be an unfair distribution of wealth. In this situation, people live within their own particular niche in society, doing their best within that niche. They only compare themselves with others who are in their own social position. They do not look outward to evaluate whether those in other social positions are better or worse off than they are. They know the characteristics of each social level, and they accept each situation as it exists.

THE RAMAYANA (PAGE 296)

1. **Bharata's nurse and mother.** The nurse changes Bharata's mother's attitude toward Rama by portraying Rama as a threat to the social position, and therefore the welfare, of her son and herself. She is preying upon the mother's vulnerable spots: a natural sense of rivalry, a sense of inferiority, and latent jealousy. Because Bharata's mother is the youngest of four wives and the mother of the second of four sons, the nurse does not have to try very hard to create fear. However, given the true nature of Rama, which is well known in

the royal family, her fears are not at all realistic, since Rama is the ideal human being.

The response of Bharata's mother is realistic because fear is emotional and often irrational. Once a person has reason to be concerned about the welfare of loved ones, he or she may take extreme action in order to preserve that welfare.

2. **Dasa-ratha.** Dasa-ratha puts himself in a position from which he feels he cannot retreat by promising his favorite wife whatever she asks for before hearing what she plans to request. He could have retreated by evaluating the reasons he had chosen Rama over Bharata and the obligations he owed to the people of his kingdom. The favor she reminded him that he owed her gave him the reason he needed to justify to himself why he was giving in to her wishes.

3. **Lakshmana and Rama.** Students' opinions may vary. The four sons of Dasa-ratha are all unusually fine human beings, as they should be, considering that they are all forms of Vishnu. Lakshmana is younger, more emotional, and less rigid than Rama. His reaction is the one that we would expect of Rama, and the contrast between his reaction and Rama's serves to enhance the perfection of Rama.

4. **Rama's obedience to his father.** Students' opinions may vary. Rama's behavior reveals the esteem in which a father is held in Hindu society, and in may societies the decree of a king would be honored even after his death. When Rama behaves as he does, he willingly undergoes deprivation, but he leaves the kingdom in able hands. He also causes Bharata's mother to feel guilty. He probably causes less of a problem in his family and in the kingdom by leaving than by contesting his father's decree.

5. **Sita's accompanying Rama into exile.** Lakshmana's behavior implies that his obligation to his brother is greater than his obligation to his wife. Another possibility is that Sita may want to go with Rama more than Lakshmana's wife wants to go with Lakshmana. Rama tells Sita that her dharma is to remain with the family, but she disagrees. Sita's behavior, when contrasted with the behavior of Lakshmana's wife, may point up the perfection of Sita as a human being and as a wife; Lakshmana's wife may not feel as Sita does.

6. **Bharata's treatment of his mother.** Students' opinions may vary. Like Lakshmana, Bharata differs from Rama in that he is younger, more emotional, and less rigid. His behavior, when contrasted with Rama's, reveals Rama's perfection. It also reveals how his mother's actions should be interpreted and proves that Lakshmana's reactions were well founded. Bharata's mother has, indeed, acted unjustly, and Rama's banishment is unfair and unjustified.

Bharata's treatment of his mother also reveals the character of Bharata himself. He does not feel threatened by Rama, and he will not take Rama's rightful position even if it is thrust upon him. Bharata considers his obligation (dharma) to his brother more important than his obligation to his mother, particularly since his mother acted improperly. Rama does not support Bharata's mother, but he advises his brother to forgive her. Bharata's mother does not anticipate her son's response because she has been caught up in her irrational fears and has lost touch with the reality of the situation.

7. **Why Bharata pleads with Rama to take throne.** Bharata knows that the kingdom is rightfully Rama's. Dharma dictates that, in this situation, he must support his brother rather than his mother, because his mother's behavior was improper.

8. **Dharma.** Students' responses may vary. Valmiki may well intend to show that Rama is the greatest of the four brothers because he behaves in the most idealistic manner. He may also intend to show that Rama is too inflexible. One would think that a variety of justifiable responses is possible in a complicated situation where a person must try to reconcile a number of conflicting obligations.

   In this part of the story, the reactions of Lakshmana and Bharata reflect the reactions of the typical reader, who may wonder why Rama accepts an unfair and intolerable situation without the slightest protest. Valmiki may have made the brothers react as they do so that they will perform this dramatic function. This behavior of Rama's may be admirable here, but the same kind of behavior later, in his treatment of Sita, is less admirable. Rama's very perfection becomes an imperfection.

9. **Rama's weapons.** Divine or magical weapons enhance a hero's stature. The gods give him such weapons as testimony to his greatness. However, such weapons may detract from his heroism because they may bring the hero a victory that he could not achieve on his own. In Rama's case the enemy also possesses divine weapons, so the battle is more evenly matched.

10. **Teasing of Ravana's sister.** Rama's teasing of Ravana's sister may be the only time Rama acts like an ordinary human being. It is quite possible that the Hindus took earlier stories of Rama and molded them to conform to the Hindu view of life. If that is indeed the case, then this incident has remained from one of the pre-Hindu versions of the myth. As the Hindus have portrayed Rama, it is most unusual for Rama to treat someone as he treats Ravana's sister.

11. **Character of Sita.** Sita remains a sympathetic character while she is treating Lakshmana unfairly because her great love of Rama and her fear for his safety motivate her behavior.

12. **Temptation of Sita.** Ravana appeals to Sita's vanity and tries to make her feel that she is being undervalued and poorly treated. Ravana offers Sita value in terms of power, glory, and material possessions.

13. **Role of monkeys.** The monkeys are appealing allies because they are very human, supportive, and clever. They add variety to the myth because they can perform feats that human beings cannot. They take the place of magic.

14. **Hanuman.** Hanuman's ability to choose his own death makes it possible for him to take more risks since he need have no fear of death. Therefore, his gift makes him both more and less heroic. He accomplishes greater deeds, but he can accomplish them without fear for his own well-being.

15. **Ravana's brothers.** Students' opinions may vary. Both Kumbha-karna and Vibhishana were correct to express their points of view without fearing the consequences.

16. **Depiction of Rakshasas.** Valmiki's portrayal of Kumbha-karna and Vibhishana makes the Rakshasas seem human. Clearly, the Rakshasas are not all evil creatures, even if they are the enemy. One evaluates them individual by individual and respects and admires many of them as one respects and admires both Greeks and Trojans in the Trojan War. Such an objective point of view enhances the quality of the myth because it is more realistic. It also makes the issues more complex and therefore more interesting.

17. **Vibhishana.** When Ravana does not agree with Vibhishana's point of view, he makes it easy for Vibhishana by banishing him. If Ravana had not done this, Vibhishana would have had to decide whether he could support his brother in an unjustified war. If he had chosen to leave, his people would have considered him a traitor. The question of whether one has the obligation to support one's country regardless of what that country is doing is important to all people.

18. **Kumbha-karna.** Kumbha-karna is portrayed humorously in the outlandish effort needed to awaken him. Humor is a delightful change of pace in a very serious epic. Kumbha-karna is to be taken seriously, however, because he is a very great warrior and he has intelligent reasons for participating in the war. Valmiki presents him as being serious and thoughtful as well as extraordinarily skillful in battle. He never loses control of himself. He respects the ability of Lakshmana and chooses not to fight him, when he could have fought and killed Lakshmana and then gone on to fight Rama.

19. **Character of Lakshmana.** Lakshmana is an impressive character. He chooses to save Vibhishana's life at great risk to his own. It enhances Lakshmana's portrayal to see that he is genuinely considerate to a number of people, and not just to Rama and Sita.

20. **Ravana as hero.** Rama gives Ravana a hero's funeral because Ravana was a very great leader. He had even conquered many of the gods. When one great leader respects another, it enhances the leader who gives respect as well as the one who receives it, for it takes a secure human being to be generous in praising the greatness of someone else, particularly a competitor.

21. **First renunciation of Sita.** Students' opinions may vary. Rama is putting his obligations as a king before his personal wishes and his obligation to his wife.

22. **Sita's response.** Sita's support of Rama's behavior may mean that it was acceptable and justified under the circumstances. Personally, however, she

must resent it because she is innocent. She might think that it was the obligation of a husband to defend his wife's innocence publicly rather than to force her to prove her innocence.

23. **Second renunciation of Sita.** Students' opinions may vary. Sita does not feel that she should be tried for the same crime twice, and many will agree with her. She has already proved her innocence.

24. **Justification for Rama's behavior.** Students' opinions may vary. Rama forces Sita to prove her innocence again because he sees his obligation to his people as bowing to their will even when they are wrong. Some may believe that he is abdicating his position as leader when he does this.

25. **Sita's revenge.** Sita is outraged, and most students probably will feel that her revenge is justified.

26. **Rama and Sita as model couple.** Students' answers may vary. Rama and Sita represent traditional models of behavior in which the husband's primary responsibility is to his community and the wife's primary responsibility is to her husband.

27. **Values in marriage.** Students' answers will vary.

28. **Rama as hero.** Rama is a great hero because he consistently puts the needs and wishes of others before his own needs and wishes. He resists the temptation to take the power that is rightfully his and to accept his wife no matter what others think of her behavior. He makes her clear her own name for the good of her own reputation as well as for his own reputation as king. He defeats the Rakshasas, who act aggressively and lawlessly in the forests, making them unsafe for hermits, holy men, and travelers.

    However, both Rama's superiority and his flaw are that he is overzealous in his desire to behave most righteously. His greatest strength is his greatest weakness. In spite of Bharata's and Lakshmana's advice, Rama quietly accepts improper criticism and behavior from others when he could defend himself. Opinion may vary as to whether he should do this. Rama's tests appear to be more important than his tasks because they reveal what kind of a human being Rama is, rather than simply demonstrating that he performs great deeds.

29. **Rama versus Bharata and Lakshmana.** Rama is a greater hero than Bharata and Lakshmana because he does what he feels he must do regardless of the personal cost. The fact that he is not perfect makes him appealingly human and therefore makes it easier for the ordinary human being to try to emulate his behavior.

Supplementary Suggestions
1. If your class has read *The Iliad* or *Sigurd the Volsung,* consider how the plot of those epics would change if each of the major characters behaved according to the principle of dharma.

2. Compare Hindu values with those of the Greeks and the Northern Europeans. Consider how each society measures greatness in a human being.

THE CREATION OF THE UNIVERSE AND HUMAN BEINGS (PAGE 324)

1. **Difference between myths of Yin and Yang and Nu Kua.** Unlike Pan Ku, Yin and Yang are not anthropomorphic divinities in that they do not possess human characteristics, either in form or personality. In contrast to Pan Ku, Yin and Yang symbolize abstract qualities.

2. **Yin and Yang: Divinity and human beings.** The myth of Yin and Yang reveals no relationship between divinity and human beings. Yin and Yang form the universe without attempting to improve life on earth. Moreover, once the universe is created, they have finished their work. They do not concern themselves with human life and a code of moral human behavior. Human life exists in an established universe in which neither divine rewards nor divine punishments exist. Therefore, sacrifice and prayer would not bring results.

3. **Nu Kua.** Nu Kua has a creative intelligence. She surveys nature with a mind that notices details, both great and small, and she can imagine what it lacks and how to create it. Her lively mind tires of one kind of creative process, so she tries another method. She is satisfied that the two processes create somewhat different products. This aspect of the myth explains why all people are not equally intelligent and equally wealthy.

4. **P'an Ku.** P'an Ku is an intelligent, industrious, and unselfish creator. He decides what he wants to do and does it, with infinite patience, determination, and perseverance. He likely would be the same kind of human being. It would be wise to give him any job that he wanted to do and that he could do well, because he would give it his best effort and would accomplish it, no matter how long it took and no matter what the obstacles.

Supplementary Suggestion

1. Consider Kung Kung's role in this myth and how he represents the nature of evil in the universe. Compare this view of evil with the view in other cultures.

CHI LI SLAYS THE SERPENT (PAGE 330)

1. **Chi Li's secret motive.** Students may have a variety of answers. Chi Li may fear failure and think that it is better to prepare her parents for the probable outcome of her encounter with the Yung serpent. She may believe that her family would be more upset by her plan than by the version that she decides to tell them. As it is, she disregards their feelings and proceeds secretly with her plan.

2. **Encouragement of Chi Li's parents.** Then and now, most parents prefer a live child to a dead hero. However, it is possible that, in our own time and

place, Chi Li's parents would be encouraged by the fact that she has a plan to slay the serpent and that she does not intend simply to submit to her death as a human sacrifice. Then and now, parents would also be proud of a daughter who wants to do something heroic for the welfare of her community.

3. **Examples of Chi Li's heroic qualities.** *Courage:* She volunteers to be a sacrifice and risks what appears to be certain death. *Creative intelligence:* She conceives of the idea of tempting (and distracting) the serpent with rice-balls that she has moistened with malt sugar. *Determination:* When her parents object to her sacrifice, she secretly volunteers. *Unselfishness:* She volunteers to sacrifice herself for the well-being of her family. *Ambition:* She determines to be a hero by devising a strategy to kill the serpent. *Strength and skill:* She stabs and kills the serpent.

4. **How gods would have blessed Chi Li.** The gods would be equated with the good luck that led the serpent to be distracted by the sugar-flavored rice-balls, that let the serpent-hound's attack against the serpent be successful, and that enabled Chi Li to think of her plan, convince the authorities to let her attempt it, and kill the serpent.

5. **Attitude toward the serpent's victims.** Chi Li thinks the other victims should have made an attempt to kill the serpent before it killed them because they had had time to devise a plan and they had nothing to lose—since they would be losing their lives if they did nothing to combat the serpent.

    Student opinion will probably vary as to whether Chi Li is an unusual person. What clearly is unusual is that she volunteers to be the serpent's victim. Chi Li is also unusual among the human sacrifices in that she is neither a slave nor the daughter of a criminal. Because she is a member of a loving family and her father possesses an honorable reputation, she possesses great self-esteem. This may well give her the courage to approach her life in the manner that she does.

    The social position of the other maiden-sacrifices has given them much less reason to respect themselves, and they probably lacked the self-esteem that Chi Li possesses. Although they had also faced certain death, they had had no choice in their fate, and this may have combined with their lack of self-esteem to make it more likely that they would have accepted the inevitability of their death instead of making any effort to avoid it.

    It is unlikely that the other maidens may have tried to kill the serpent but had failed in their attempt. Since the county officials were present to observe their deaths, these officials would have reported any courage these maidens would have displayed, and their society would have heard about it and would have looked admiringly upon them.

6. **Chi Li and Chinese society.** The myth of Chi Li reflects the attitude toward sons and daughters in Chinese society at that time. Sons were valued for the strength that they possessed—strength that was necessary to farm the fields and defend their country in time of war. Daughters could only grow up to give birth to more mouths than the land could feed.

AMATERASU (PAGE 335)

1. **Amaterasu and fertility.** Amaterasu separates the sun and the moon. When her messenger brings her the foods of the earth, she plants each group of seeds in the appropriate location and appoints a divine village chief to supervise their growth. She invents the art of raising silkworms. Because of these efforts, human beings have what they need in order to survive.

2. **Susano-o-no-Mikoto's visit.** Amaterasu lets her brother remain with her because she believes him when he says that he will not remain long and that he will cause her no trouble. Because he is her brother, she does not banish him. Instead, she gives him opportunities to behave properly.

Supplementary Suggestion
1. Consider whether it matters that Susano-o-no-Mikoto is not a monster and what his behavior implies in terms of the nature of evil in the universe.

KOTAN UTUNNAI (PAGE 339)

1. **Narrator as hero.** Students' opinions may vary. This technique increases the element of surprise because the reader never knows more than the narrator does.

2. **Narrator's youth.** The narrator's youth is unusual in that he is raised by a stranger in a strange community without realizing who he really is. It increases the element of surprise in the myth.

3. **Narrator's heroic tasks.** The narrator kills Repunkur warriors wherever he finds them. He also kills the storm demon and the demon's sister. The trials faced by the narrator include whether or not he will harm the woman who reared him and Shipish-un-mat since they are his family's enemy. In each case the narrator evaluates the woman as an individual rather than as a member of a group, he respects her abilities, and he treats her in a humane way.

4. **Older Sister.** Older Sister is an unusually courageous and independent young woman. Not only is she a fine warrior, but she has the courage and sensitivity to rescue an infant of an enemy people when his parents are killed and then leave her own people in order to raise him in safety.

5. **Older Sister's warning.** Students' opinions may vary. Older Sister may fear for her own safety once she tells the narrator that her people killed his parents.

6. **Acquiring heroic qualities.** The narrator gains the heroic qualities of his father by putting on his father's clothes, armor, and sword. In our society, young people may feel that they are gaining the qualities of an admired relative or friend when they wear something that belongs to that person.

7. **Shipish-un-kur.** Shipish-un-kur is different from what the Repunkur warriors say about him in that he is an honorable man who is slow to anger and

not bloodthirsty. He fights against the gods but not against human beings. He has no intention of fighting the narrator but intends to greet him in peace and treat him with kindness. Students' opinions will vary as to whether this is a realistic attitude.

8. **Magical qualities.** The narrator is able to make himself invisible and fight without being seen. He can also fly through the air like a bird. Older Sister, Shipish-un-kur, Shipish-un-mat, and Kamui-otupus can also fly through the air, as can Dangling Nose. Magical attributes enhance the heroic quality of those who possess them.

9. **Divine versus human.** The only difference between those who are divine and those who are mortal appears to be whether or not the person can die. Beings can make themselves appear and disappear, and some of them can shed one form and emerge in another—as a snake sheds its skin. It appears from the case of Older Sister that the gods can and will restore to life someone who has died.

10. **Gods and warriors.** The narrator gets the gods to come to his aid by promising them the blood of the Repunkur to gorge upon, which is more blood than the narrator himself possesses. This incident suggests that the warriors of that culture drank the blood of the enemies they killed in order to gain their courage, strength, and skill.

11. **Restoration to life.** It appears from the case of Older Sister that the gods will reward those beings who have lived a meritorious life with a return to life after they die. The east is often the direction of life because the sun, bringer of life and fertility to the soil, rises in the east. Similarly, the west is often the direction of death because the sun sets or dies in the west.

12. **Shipish-un-mat's behavior.** Students' opinions may vary. Many students will feel that Shipish-un-mat acts properly when she turns against her brother because he repeatedly tries to kill her while the narrator is using her as a shield. Shipish-un-kur's behavior is unexpectedly callous and cruel, considering how proud he was of his kindness to human beings.

13. **Why Shipish-un-mat helps narrator.** Shipish-un-mat is in a difficult position. She is actually such a fine warrior that she might have made it very difficult for the narrator to succeed while he was using her as a shield. Then her brother would have protected her. As it is, her brother's behavior so angers her that as soon as the narrator releases her, she attacks her brother. She could have taken that opportunity to escape from the narrator and bring warriors to the aid of her brother. Given her social position, it is not realistic to assume that she could have joined another community and thus avoided taking sides.

14. **Character of narrator.** The narrator is a courageous, proud, competitive, broad-minded young man who is a skilled warrior. He fights all the Repunkur bravely and well. He is motivated to seek out Shipish-un-kur and fight with him in order to prove his own excellence.

His only fault seems to be that he cannot resist the temptation to prove himself in a contest with another warrior who has a great reputation. This need to prove himself is more important than the fact that, by so doing, he is provoking someone who does not intend to be his enemy to fight against him. As a result of their battle, the king's sister becomes alienated from her brother and fights against him, the narrator's brother joins the narrator in the ensuing battle, and many people are needlessly slaughtered.

However, given the need for a warrior to be courageous, strong, and skilled in battle, it is understandable that the hero would have sought out Shipish-un-kur in order to establish his own greatness. Moreover, in his defense as a human being, the narrator accepts and appreciates both Older Sister and Shipish-un-mat, even though they are from enemy peoples, because they are such good human beings and fine warriors. His lack of prejudice makes him unusually admirable and very appealing. The fact that the hero is not perfect makes him a realistic and an appealing figure.

15. **Most sympathetic character.** Because the characters are so well drawn, students' opinions will vary. Conceivably, the narrator is least appealing because he initiates the fight with Shipish-un-kur. Attitudes will vary toward Shipish-un-kur and Shipish-un-mat depending upon whether students feel that Shipish-un-mat did all she could do for her brother while the narrator used her as a shield.

16. **Shipish-un-mat's value.** The narrator values Shipish-un-mat's great beauty and her equally great courage and skill in battle. He marries the sister of his enemy because her family matters less to him than her qualities as an individual. Since the narrator reacts to Older Sister in the same way, the reader is prepared for his lack of prejudice.

Supplementary Suggestion

1. If your students have read *The Iliad,* you may want to compare it and *Kotan Utunnai* in terms of the setting, the cause of the war, the type of justice, the motivation of a hero, and the values held by each society.

THE CREATION CYCLE (PAGE 351)

1. **Maori gods.** The Maori gods have human emotions and behave in ways that are characteristic of human beings. For example, they exhibit love, jealousy, and the desire to use retribution as a way of dealing with their grievances. The myths emphasize the war as a characteristic of nature and the natural predilection of many human beings to wage war as a way to achieve their goals.

2. **Greatest natural enemy.** The greatest natural enemy of the Maori appears to be the wind, because Tawhiri overcomes every god except for Tu, god of war-spirited human beings and god of war. Moreover, Tu and Tawhiri continue to battle each other to this day, a fact that explains the predilection of human beings for war as a way of attempting to solve their problems.

3. **View of humankind.** This myth views humankind as being very warlike. Revenge, rather than solving problems through discussion, is the pervading force in the myth, and Tu is both god of war and god of the warlike spirit in human beings.

4. **Maui as trickster-hero.** Students' opinions may vary. Some students will think that Maui's being a trickster-hero adds to his heroic image in that being clever is a sign of creative intelligence. Consequently, Maui's tricks enable him to perform greater heroic feats. However, others may feel that Maui's tricks make him too humorous a figure to take seriously and that, therefore, his being a trickster detracts from his heroic image.

THE TAMING OF THE SUN (PAGE 360)

1. **Setting of myth.** The setting of this myth reflects the importance of the sun in the Hawaiian Islands for the raising of food, catching of fish, and making of clothes.

2. **Character of Maui.** This myth reveals Maui to be courageous, persevering, clever, and kind. Most students will probably like him.

3. **Role of magic.** The magic in this myth makes the myth possible. Since Maui's adversary is the sun, he would need something as powerful as magic to conquer such a formidable force. Most students will probably think that magic enhances the myth by adding interest. Others will prefer a more realistic story, even though they might find it difficult to create a realistic version of this subject.

4. **Maui as trickster-hero.** Most students will probably think that Maui's being a trickster-hero adds to his heroic image in this myth. It reveals his creative intelligence and makes it possible for him to succeed with his task.

THE BRITISH ISLES

THE AGES OF THE WORLD (PAGE 369)

1. **The Irish ages.** The Irish ages improve from the first through the fifth, the fifth being the Golden Age of Ireland. The sixth age is the age of mortals, and its description is like the age in which Hesiod lives. The description of the last age is common to many mythologies, for life in the present is always very complex and beset with problems. Although life in the agricultural age was technologically more difficult, many people look back to earlier values and prefer them.

2. **Celtic values.** The attitude of the Túatha Dé toward Bres reveals some of their values. It was important for a leader to be generous and not to tax his people in order to acquire wealth for his own private enjoyment. It was important to respect other people and to treat them accordingly. It was important to treat guests hospitably, sheltering and feeding them well. It is also clear from the myth that Celtic society contained at least two social classes. Bres, as one of the gods, was supposed to treat the Túatha Dé as gods rather than as nongods or servants, providing a model of appropriate behavior.

3. **The Túatha Dé.** The Túatha Dé reveal their divinity in the magic they can perform, such as Lug's ability to shine like the sun and his and Dagda's ability to wield magical weapons. On the other hand, the doctor's jealousy of his son is very human. The Túatha Dé's recognition of Lug's skills and their attempt to preserve his life are also human. They live like human beings who possess great skill with magic.

4. **Role of magic.** Students' opinions may vary, but magic probably enhances this myth. The Túatha Dé are the fifth race to inhabit Ireland. The earlier races did not employ magic and their experiences are much less interesting. Their magical weapons and magic tricks make the Túatha Dé memorable.

DAGDA THE GOOD (PAGE 378)

1. **Fertility gods.** Fertility of the soil seems not to have been a problem in Ireland, since both peoples who want to inhabit the land possess powers of fertility. The problem is more political than agricultural. The question is not whether the land will be fertile, but which people will control the land.

2. **Dagda.** Because the problem in Ireland is political, it is important that Dagda be a very fine warrior. Skill in warfare was necessary if the Túatha Dé were going to be able to conquer the Fomorians and have the land for themselves.

BEOWULF (PAGE 381)

1. **Role of funerals.** The mood of *Beowulf* is one of death. People live with the shadow of death hovering over their shoulders in the form of Grendel, his mother, a dragon, invasion by foreigners, or family treachery.

2. **Peace or war.** It is clear that Beowulf lives in a time of war because soldiers guard the coasts of Denmark and Geatland. The men are accustomed to sleeping with their armor and weapons by their sides, as if they must be ready to go to war at a moment's notice.

3. **Swords and values.** Warriors named their swords because their lives depended on them. The fact that swords have names and slaves do not suggests how deeply rooted the warrior culture was. Other famous heroes with named swords include Sigurd and Arthur.

4. **Unferth's drunken speech.** Unferth's speech is a way of learning what Beowulf has already accomplished in his life, for Beowulf must prove that Unferth's accusation is unjustified and unjust. Beowulf's speech is therefore the more important of the two.

   It is important to know that Unferth is the greatest hero of the Danes, because it explains why he is jealous and angry that Beowulf has arrived uninvited to solve the Danes' problem. That Unferth himself cannot solve the problem increases its size and also increases Beowulf's heroism, for when Beowulf kills Grendel, he does what the greatest of the Danish heroes is not courageous, strong, or skilled enough to do.

5. **Grendel's appearance.** Students opinions may vary as to whether the *Beowulf* poet should have described the appearance of Grendel and his mother. One of the Arthur poets describes a Grendel-like monster that Arthur kills in great, gory detail. However, to describe the fear the monster causes without describing the monster leaves the description of the monster to one's imagination. This technique may thus create an infinitely more frightening creature than the author's description could create.

6. **Beowulf and Grendel.** Students' opinions may vary as to why Beowulf permitted Grendel to kill one of his warriors. The author permitted it in order to enable the reader to watch Grendel in action. The author could have chosen to have one of Hrothgar's men describe a previous incident, but, in reality, most men would concentrate on running for their lives from such a monster rather than risking their lives to acquire a description of the event for someone else. Beowulf is not afraid and will not run, so he is the logical observer and recorder of Grendel's dreadful deeds.

   Also, it is not clear what else Beowulf could have done, other than sleep at the door to Herot so that he would have been the first to be attacked. Undoubtedly, Grendel was too quick to be stopped once he grabbed a victim, and watching Grendel in action gives Beowulf time to evaluate his enemy and plan how to deal with him.

   Most students will likely believe that Beowulf's decision is wise: by losing one man, he is better able to save the rest of the men. It would have been more heroic to sleep by the door, but it would have created a less interesting story.

7. **Grendel's mother.** Grendel's mother is stronger than her son in order to be a greater adversary for Beowulf. If she were weaker, the second battle would have been an anticlimax. Beowulf is a greater hero when he can kill a greater monster. Therefore, Grendel's mother contributes much to Beowulf's heroism. He has to swim down to the bottom of the sea with his armor on, fighting off monsters as he descends, in order to enter her den. Then he is forced to use a weapon that no one else could even lift in order to kill her. The fact that he almost loses the fight intensifies the difficulty of the fight and makes Beowulf's victory that much greater.

8. **Role of monsters.** Monsters are less common, more frightening, less predictable, and more dangerous than men are. All warriors are accustomed to fighting other warriors. Monsters present new risks and greater fear, and therefore it takes more courage, strength, and skill to kill them.

9. **Role of honor.** Students' answers may vary. Beowulf probably would have killed Grendel's mother even if Hrothgar had not honored him for killing Grendel. He would hope for greater honor and gifts after having proved himself an even greater hero. Even if the local king did not honor him, he would achieve fame that would travel.

Even if Beowulf had heard that Hrothgar was a stingy, greedy king, who gave no gifts and hoarded all wealth for himself, Beowulf probably would not have resisted the chance to prove himself a hero. Because Beowulf cared about having a heroic reputation, he would have to perform a second great deed whether or not a king rewarded him for his heroism.

10. **Incidents in Beowulf's life.** The *Beowulf* poet focuses only on the high points of Beowulf's life, namely his battles with the monsters he killed. Descriptions of other battles and the coronation ceremony would have been less interesting, and they would have slowed down the action of the story.

11. **How Beowulf changes.** The major difference between Beowulf as a young man and as an old man is psychological. The older Beowulf is less self-confident, and he does not want to die. He is less self-confident because he feels his age, and he knows that even the best of weapons will not conquer a dragon. He fears death more because it is more likely to occur now that he does not possess the physical strength he had in his youth.

The difference in his psychological attitude may well cause his death. His heroic feats have all been against such formidable foes that, without unbounded self-confidence, he never would have had the courage and strength to win.

However, in many ways Beowulf is still very much the same in old age as he was in his youth. He still fights monsters for glory and fame and to make his country safe. He still talks himself into being self-confident, and he tries his best. However, he cannot quite believe his own self-confident speech, and he knows when his best is not going to be good enough.

12. **Beowulf, Hrothgar, and Wiglaf.** Both the first and the last parts of the epic involve an old king and a young warrior who helps him. Beowulf is different from Wiglaf in that he is a greater hero. He comes to foreign shores with a band of men under his command, and he fights alone, without weapons. Beowulf is a greater king than Hrothgar because he takes it upon himself to fight the monster that is threatening his kingdom. He may die, but he will die defending his country.

13. **Beowulf and dragon.** Students' opinions may vary. Beowulf certainly wants and needs to protect his people; as king that is his obligation. He says that the dragon's treasure makes his death acceptable to him, which may be a little out of character, although Sigurd would agree with this remark. He has achieved unusual fame and glory during his lifetime, but he may fear being called a coward in his old age. Given the time in which Beowulf lived, if he had refused to fight the dragon, it is very possible that his people would have lost confidence in his ability to defend them, and the rulers of other, hostile nations would have hastened to invade Geatland.

14. **Desertion of Beowulf.** Students' opinions may vary. The desertion of Beowulf's men enhances Beowulf's heroism, because it dramatizes how fearsome the dragon actually is.

15. **Why men desert Beowulf.** Students' answers may vary. The deserters knowingly give up all claim to honor, reputation, and land because the dragon frightens them into thinking only of saving their lives.

16. **Death of Beowulf.** Beowulf dies fighting the dragon because he is outmatched, and he chooses to die fighting for a heroic cause rather than to die quietly in bed. If he were younger, he would have been more self-confident and might have been able to think of a way to kill the dragon. For example, Sigurd avoided Fafnir's flames by digging a pit and striking him from beneath, where dragons do not have scales.

17. **Attitude toward death.** Beowulf thinks less of death as a young man because the reality is farther away. He has such self-confidence that his announcement that he will risk death in order to acquire fame does not worry him. A person's attitude toward death and the feeling of fear always affect his or her performance. Fear robs a person of the ability to persevere and actually weakens physical strength. However, Beowulf's fear does not detract from his heroic image because his fear makes Beowulf a very realistic and appealing human being.

18. **Character of Beowulf.** Like Heracles, Beowulf will do whatever is necessary to make the world he lives in a safer place. Also like Heracles, he possesses incredible courage and unusual strength. He resists the temptation to ignore the dragon because, both politically and in terms of his own self-image, he cannot afford to ignore the monster. Consequently, Beowulf is one of the world's greatest heroes.

19. **Value of gold.** The attitude of the *Beowulf* poet toward gold is the same as the attitude of the *Sigurd* poet. Gold is both a blessing and a curse, depending

upon one's attitude. If it is distributed generously and used to benefit a king's nobles and his people, it is a blessing. If it is hoarded, it is a curse.

20. **Light and darkness.** It is no accident that all three monsters live in the dark: Grendel and his mother in an underwater cave and the dragon in a cave in the earth. All three monsters are nocturnal. Beowulf and other human beings live in bright sunlight. The warriors wear shining armor to protect them from all that is evil. Heorot shines in the sunlight from the metal that decorates it, and the interior walls shine from the gold threads in the hanging tapestries.

Supplementary Questions

1. According to the *Beowulf* poet, what qualities does the ideal king possess?

2. According to the *Beowulf* poet, what qualities does the ideal hero possess?

KING ARTHUR (PAGE 418)

1. **Second Troy.** In order to be taken seriously and to be allowed the privileges of an aristocrat, it was important to have a family pedigree. Epic heroes, too, needed to have a pedigree if they were to be taken seriously and esteemed highly. They had to be related to the right people—either to important gods or to important families.

   This tradition starts with the Babylonians and the Greeks and Trojans, because those epics are the oldest epics available to the Western world. Gilgamesh is two-thirds god, Achilles is the son of a goddess, and everyone else comes from a prestigious royal family. Such was the prominence of Homer's epics that Virgil based his epic on them, and such was the prominence of *The Aeneid* that Geoffrey of Monmouth made Brutus a relative of Aeneas and Priam.

2. **Stonehenge.** Geoffrey of Monmouth and the Arthur poets who followed him connected Arthur's family with Stonehenge because the Celts were important in Britain and were worthy relatives for an aristocrat. To the extent that early kings of Britain were thought to be buried at Stonehenge, it was important to relate Arthur to these kings.

3. **Proofs of kingship.** It is necessary to have proof of legitimate title to kingship because in each country a number of aristocrats are always powerful enough to usurp a throne, and no king can rule without their support. A king needs to be able to prove why he, as opposed to some other aristocrat, deserves the right to be king. Having a god choose the king, which Odin does when he plunges into the tree the sword that only Sigmund can remove, is a noteworthy and respected method. Merlin functions in that capacity when he causes the sword in the stone to appear in the churchyard.

4. **Character of Merlin.** Students' opinions may vary. Most people enjoy Merlin's ability to foresee the future and to perform magic.

5. **Merlin's flaws.** Students' opinions may vary. Merlin's blind spots do make him a very human figure, with human limitations. They also create a much more interesting story. They may also indicate that the unexpected is a part of life that cannot be removed, even by the most talented of men. With this in mind, Merlin's flaws do not detract from his image, because perfection is impossible for anyone to attain.

6. **Excalibur.** Arthur's sword has a name for the same reason that Sigurd's and Beowulf's swords do. Warfare was a common pursuit in the Middle Ages, and a warrior's life depended upon his sword. Excalibur also has an unusual sheath, and Arthur receives it in an unusual way, both serving to emphasize its importance. Only a famous hero possessed a great sword, so a named sword reflected favorably upon the reputation of the hero who possessed it.

7. **Arthur's heroic tasks.** Arthur is created to be the superhero of heroes. Whatever any other hero in the history of the Western world has done, Arthur must do. In order to compete with Alexander the Great, Arthur conquers the Roman Empire and becomes its emperor. Like Beowulf, he defeats a monstrous, Grendel-like giant. Less imposing, but with greater practical importance, he successfully conquers all British kings who oppose his rule, and he frees Britain from the Saxons who have plagued the land since Ambrosius and Uther were king.

8. **Prophecy about Guinevere.** Students' opinions may vary. The prophecy functions as foreshadowing. Arthur is unwise to ignore the prophecy because Merlin turns out to be correct. However, Arthur's behavior is understandable: most people disregard warnings of doom when they contradict what a person really wants to do.

9. **Arthur and Guinevere.** The marriage of Guinevere and Arthur is probably a political one. Royal marriages usually were political alliances, and the original versions of the Arthur myth include no romantic details, which is why this version is also sparse on this topic. While it is uncertain whether Guinevere learns to love Arthur, she is loyal to him until she falls in love with Lancelot.

10. **Lancelot as knight.** Lancelot is the greatest knight in King Arthur's court because he is the best fighter and is the most courteous in terms of fighting fairly and in terms of his treatment of all females. His treatment of Sir Gawain at the end of the story shows Lancelot acting in a noble way even though he had every reason to hate Gawain. Lancelot's treatment of other ladies reveals his loyalty to Guinevere. However, his reputation as the greatest knight is ironic because his love of Guinevere causes him to be disloyal to Arthur in spite of the fact that a true knight's first duty is to his king.

11. **Character of Lancelot.** Lancelot would not be an appealing character or elicit sympathy if he were not such a good human being. His good intentions make him a tragic figure. Lancelot tries to be the best at every task he undertakes and to carry out every responsibility of the true knight. He wants to be the best knight both to Arthur and to Guinevere, and it is not possible to be

both. He is forced to choose, and given his great love for Guinevere, which she reciprocates, he chooses the queen over the king. His crime affects his heroic image because he is not strong enough to give up loving Guinevere when it is in the best interest of Arthur, Guinevere, Britain, and himself that he do so.

12. **Arthur as king.** Arthur is the ideal king in that he puts the needs of his country before his own needs and feelings. Arthur condones Guinevere's relationship with Lancelot as long as he can in order to preserve the Round Table and the unity of Britain. He has the self-control that Lancelot lacks, which enhances his heroic image.

13. **Guinevere's infidelity.** Agravain and Mordred are unwise to confront Arthur with Guinevere's infidelity. Gawain is right when he tells them that by so doing they will destroy the Round Table and, with it, the unity of Britain.

14. **Arthur's response to love affair.** The fact that Arthur ignores the love affair between Guinevere and Lancelot until Agravain and Mordred make a public issue of it reflects great psychological strength. The love affair between his wife and one of his two favorite knights causes him great anguish, yet Arthur steadfastly puts the needs of Britain before his own needs and feelings.

15. **Why Guinevere refuses to flee.** Guinevere refuses to flee with Lancelot because she feels an obligation to Arthur as her husband and king.

16. **Gawain.** Gawain's reputation is obviously still great. Arthur, Lancelot, and the other knights hold him in high esteem. He is the defender of proper behavior. He will not side with Agravain and Mordred, who are his brothers, when it is in the best interests of Arthur and his country that he not do so. He defends Guinevere to Arthur when she clearly appears to be guilty. He is a great fighter in his own right, possessing magical powers that would only be given to the greatest of men. Gawain only changes when Lancelot inadvertently kills his younger brothers, and then his desire for retributive justice blinds him to what the loyal and intelligent knight would advise his king to do.

17. **Mordred.** Students' opinions may vary. The original versions of the Arthur myth are sketchy about Mordred, just as they are sketchy about Guinevere. He is presented as a jealous knight who wants Guinevere for himself and who wants Britain as well. Arthur appears to treat Mordred as well as he treats anyone else. None of the original authors deals with the effects of Mordred's bastard birth upon his personality or upon his life in Margawses and Lot's family. He appears to be an evil person, who is jealous, ambitious, and disloyal. He must also be a demagogue because he manages to convince enough Britons that Arthur is a bad king and to rally a huge army to his side.

18. **Lancelot and Guinevere.** Guinevere's love for Lancelot is tragic, because she desires to be loyal to Arthur as well as to him. She hurts Arthur unintentionally because she is not strong enough to give up the man she truly loves. Lancelot's love for Guinevere is tragic, because he wants to be the best knight

both to Arthur and to Guinevere. However, he finds that he must choose between two people he loves, and he is not strong enough to give up his love for Guinevere. Their love is doubly tragic in that it causes the destruction of the Round Table and Arthur's kingdom.

19. **How characters change.** Students' opinions may vary. (a) Arthur is a great king as long as he makes independent judgments. He is wrong to follow Merlin's advice about drowning the infants. He is wrong to follow Gawain's advice and fight Lancelot. Once he is publicly faced with Guinevere and Lancelot's affair, he makes judgments that are not in the best interest of his country. Later he is very sorry, but the situation is beyond his ability to control. (b) and (c) Lancelot and Guinevere put their love for each other before their obligation to Arthur and to Britain because they cannot give one another up. When this causes a national catastrophe, Guinevere repents and gives up Lancelot. Her strength gives him no choice but to leave her, and at the end of his life, he too repents. (d) Gawain is the ideal knight, loyal to his king and his queen until Lancelot inadvertently kills his younger brothers. Then his desire for blood vengeance makes him blind to what he owes his king and queen. His advice to Arthur and his relentless pursuit of Lancelot destroys the kingdom, and it kills him. At the end of his life, he realizes what damage his blindly emotional behavior has caused. (e) Mordred changes from a knight who ostensibly is loyal to Arthur to one who is a traitor.

20. **Appeal of characters.** Students' opinions about Lancelot, Guinevere, and Arthur may vary. All are appealing characters because they try to act honorably and loyally to one another. Their intentions are good, but none of them can cope with Lancelot and Guinevere's great love for each other.

21. **Broken truce.** Students' opinion may vary. The snake incident is a realistic touch. As long as human beings or animals are involved, something unpredictable can happen that may change the course of events.

22. **Arthur's mysterious death.** The conclusion to the epic is appealing because it keeps open the possibility that Arthur is still alive and will return when Britain needs him. It permits the epic to have what might be only a temporary conclusion, with the possibility of a sequel of events to follow.

Supplementary Suggestion
1. Discuss what aspects of this myth make it popular in contemporary American society.

NORTHERN EUROPE

THE CREATION, DEATH, AND REBIRTH
OF THE UNIVERSE (PAGE 459)

1. **How myths reflect life.** These myths were written down in Iceland, which is a land of fiery volcanic action, waterfalls, and ice. The northern environment is cold and harsh, with long, dark winters and short summers of long days. It is a land of extremes: hot and cold, dark and light, fertile soil and bare rock. It is therefore not surprising that the people who lived in such lands would see many forces in nature as evil and unfriendly.

2. **Gods like humans.** The Norse gods are like human beings in that they think, speak, and act like intelligent people. Gangleri visits them and converses as he would with a teacher. He is not surprised by their appearance, and he does not doubt their willingness or their ability to explain the answers to his questions. He learns that, like wealthy human beings, the gods live in palaces, with grown children living in separate buildings from their parents. Like mortals, the gods have enemies, the Frost Giants, and they have a watchman to help preserve their safety.

3. **Ragnarok.** Ragnarok explains what happened to the Norse gods and to the giants, as well. These myths were written down by monks for people who no longer believed in the gods, and the creation myth explains how things used to be and why life is better now. By 1000 A.D., the peoples of Northern Europe possessed greater technological skills and therefore were better prepared to survive in their environment. Once that happened, nature became less threatening; the giants had died.

   Ragnarok reflects aspects of early European society. Aggressive people lived in Northern Europe, and many of their ways were as harsh as their environment. Tribe warred against tribe, burning, pillaging, and murdering in the process. Ragnarok also reflects aspects of the Northern European climate and environment. Winters brought severe winds, frost, and snow, and by March, they must have seemed interminable.

THE DEATH OF BALDER (PAGE 467)

1. **Why Loki kills Balder.** Balder's invulnerability may have been sufficient reason for Loki to kill him. Certainly, Loki could have resented that Balder possessed a quality that he himself did not possess. However, it is even more possible that Loki hated Balder because he was jealous of the kind of god Balder was. Because he was the most gentle and kind of beings, everyone and everything in the universe loved Balder. Few felt that way about Loki. To Loki, Balder was a constant reminder of everything that Loki was not. In fact, Balder's goodness so irritated Loki that it was worth being punished to get rid of him.

2. **Hel and Balder.** Hel does not expect that she will have to free Balder, because she knows that her father, Loki, will never say that he loves Balder. This myth reveals that none of the Norse gods is omnipotent. Even Odin, who sacrificed one of his eyes in order to learn about the future, cannot change that future. Loki may represent the evil that exists in the world that nothing can eradicate, like Set in the Osiris myth.

3. **Why myth is famous.** Students' opinions may vary. The age-old desire to avoid death, the great appeal of Balder's goodness, the love the gods have for him, the existence of an enemy who is as creative as he is evil, and the triumph of good over evil all help to explain its appeal.

Supplementary Conceptss
1. Students who are familiar with Greek mythology may assume that all gods are immortal. While this is indeed true in Greek mythology, it is obviously not true in Norse mythology, where the gods possess a limited form of immortality. They live until Ragnarok, and the death of Balder ushers in the period in which the gods will die. You may wish to discuss the different world views reflected by cultures that created mortal or immortal gods.

2. When the guard at the bridge asks Hermod the name of his father, he is performing a common practice of the time. The good and evil deeds of a father were inherited by his children, and a child was helped or hurt by the reputation of his or her father. In a time when wars and treachery were commonplace, the stranger had to convince guards of his identity and his goodwill. The child of a famous father, known for his good deeds, was trusted. A child whose father was unknown might be turned away. Students may find it interesting to discuss how family identity plays a role in modern life.

THE THEFT OF THOR'S HAMMER (PAGE 475)

1. **Character of Thor.** Thor would be a big, burly human being who possesses great physical strength and a personality that could express great anger or great humor. Everything about Thor appears to be great, including his appetite. As the defender of the gods, he is a very appealing character.

2. **Role of humor.** This myth is unusual in that humor is its outstanding virtue. It reveals that the people who lived in the harsh lands of the north and who often treated strangers and enemies with cruelty possessed imagination and a sense of humor. Consequently, we are able to find something that we like about them.

   Students may be able to suggest other humorous myths that they have read. Myths in *World Mythology* that have a humorous element include "Dagda the Good," the Maui myths, "Lodge-Boy and Thrown-Away," the Raven myth, and "Caught by a Hair-String."

SIGURD THE VOLSUNG (PAGE 478)

1. **Sigurd's tasks.** Sigurd's greatest feats are slaying the dragon Fafnir and thereby winning his treasure and rescuing Brunhild. He also kills Regin, but this is secondary because it was not as difficult to do. In the complete epic, Sigurd fights as valiantly in the wars as Gunnar does, but such deeds are less extraordinary.

2. **Sigurd and Gunnar.** Sigurd is more heroic than Gunnar because he performs more difficult and more dangerous deeds. However, while the nature of a person's deeds determines his or her heroism, they do not determine the quality of that person as a human being. Sigurd is a greater human being than Gunnar because he is a loyal husband to Gudrun and friend to Gunnar even though he is in love with Brunhild. Sigurd would never have treated Gunnar as Gunnar treats Sigurd, even for Brunhild's sake. He is the stronger, more secure, and more honorable person.

3. **Prophecies.** Students' opinions may vary. Usually, the story remains just as exciting, because a prophecy is a skeleton, and the details of the plot become the clothing. An infinite variety of clothing is possible, and that is never revealed to the reader in advance.

4. **Fafnir's treasure hoard.** Sigurd takes Fafnir's cursed treasure because he values it and feels that, being mortal, his destiny is death no matter what other choices he makes. The good life is one in which a person has performed courageous deeds and has won glory, honor, fame, and treasure. Sigurd admires Fafnir for capturing the treasure and keeping it until he died, and he will settle for that much in his own life.

    Students' opinions may vary as to whether it is a mistake for Sigurd to take the treasure. If he had not taken it, he would not have roasted the dragon's heart and tasted its blood. He also probably would not have killed Regin. He would not have understood the language of the birds, who told him about Brunhild, and he would not have rescued her. Thus, he would have missed meeting the great love of his life. On the other hand, had he not found Brunhild and given her Fafnir's cursed ring, the incident with Gunnar and Gudrun that led to his own death may never have occurred.

5. **Value of gold.** Those who created this myth considered gold to be both good and evil. It is good in that it brings wealth and luxury. It is evil in that it creates envy and leads to dreadful crimes. Few people can resist the temptations of gold, and the person who has it must take extra care not to let the gold affect his or her values.

6. **Deception of Sigurd and Brunhild.** Sigurd is tricked when Grimhild gives Sigurd a drugged potion that makes him forget Brunhild. In time he falls in love with Gudrun and marries her. Brunhild is tricked when Gunnar and Sigurd change appearances, so that Sigurd will look like Gunnar when he rides through the flames to Brunhild a second time. Brunhild thinks that Gunnar has rescued her until Gudrun tells her the truth.

Sigurd is a far kinder, more understanding, and honorable person than Brunhild is. At Brunhild's wedding, the effects of the potion wear off, and he remembers his love for her. He also realizes exactly how he has been tricked. However, he does nothing about it. He will not hurt his wife and his best friend, even though he still loves his best friend's wife.

In contrast, when Brunhild realizes the truth, she has no qualms about hurting others. She sets Gunnar against Sigurd and inspires him to plot Sigurd's death. The deed sets Gudrun against her brothers. Death follows upon death from then on.

7. **Character of Sigurd.** It is interesting that the only temptations Sigurd does not resist are the ones that lead to heroism: killing Fafnir, taking his treasure, and attempting to rescue Brunhild twice. Even though he loves Brunhild, he resists hurting his wife and Gunnar and causing interfamily strife. The fact that a magic potion forced him to forget Brunhild excuses him from being unfaithful. The fact that the temptations he resists keep him from hurting good people makes him a very appealing human being. The fact that he cannot resist performing heroic deeds makes him a great hero.

8. **Sigurd as hero.** The major mistake Sigurd makes in the epic is to help Gunnar by tricking Brunhild. He does not realize that he is tricking the woman he loves when he does this, but he should not have done it anyway. It is a form of cheating that permits Brunhild to think that Gunnar has performed deeds that he never could have performed on his own. While some students may believe that deceiving Brunhild undermines his character, others may believe that his magical abilities enhance his heroic stature. Also, in Sigurd's ignorance of who Brunhild is, he is simply doing his best to help his best friend. His good intentions are misguided, but they do preserve his heroic reputation.

9. **Heroes and perfection.** It is always good that a hero is not perfect. Imperfection makes heroism attainable for ordinary people.

10. **Treachery and death.** This epic is filled with characters who commit harmful deeds for justifiable reasons. For example, Hreidmar refuses to divide Andvari's treasure with Fafnir and Regin, and that is why Fafnir kills his father. Regin directs Sigurd to kill Fafnir in order to regain his share of the treasure. Sigurd kills Fafnir because the treasure had made him evil; he kills Regin in self-defense to prevent Regin from killing him. Grimhild gives Sigurd the potion because she admires him and wants him to marry her daughter. Sigurd rescues Brunhild for Gunnar because Gunnar is his best friend. Gudrun tells Brunhild the truth because Brunhild acts arrogantly toward her. Brunhild demands vengeance because Sigurd inadvertently tricked her into marrying the lesser of the two men. Gunnar plots to kill Sigurd because he desperately loves his wife and wants to please her. Guttorm kills Sigurd because he has been drugged.

Supplementary Suggestions

1. Depending on the other epics you have had your class read, students may find it interesting to compare Brunhild and Dido or to compare Sigurd with Gilgamesh and Beowulf.

2. You may wish to compare retributive justice, the role of fate, and the use of magic in various epics.

AFRICA

THE CREATION OF THE UNIVERSE AND IFE (PAGE 509)

1. **Creation of human beings.** Obatala and Olorun create human beings in order to have friends in Ife. This implies a close relationship between the gods and human beings, one of caring, sharing, and other aspects of friendship.

2. **Explanation of disabilities.** The explanation for the existence of deformed people shows a sensitivity to the needs of those who are different from the majority. This sensitivity and compassion is also evident in Obatala's promise to protect anyone who is deformed. These are superb values because they affirm each human being, in spite of differences between individuals. Our society is devoting increasing attention to making the lives of disabled people easier and richer through improved access to locations and opportunities.

THE ORIGIN OF LIFE AND FIRE (PAGE 515)

1. **Myth and culture.** This myth reflects the birds and animals that are indigenous to their particular location.

2. **Nature of Bumba and his universe.** Bumba is a beneficent god. He creates a universe that is basically good, and then it is important to him that the human beings whom he has created appreciate the world in which they live and that they live in peace with all that lives. Bumba also watches over his creations and acts like a culture hero. When human beings need fire, it is Bumba who is sympathetic and who teaches them how to make it.

3. **Nature and purpose of human beings.** Bumba has created human beings to live and let live. He would have them thrive on earth without hurting each other. It is possible that part of their purpose is to appreciate all that he has created.

4. **Bumba's visits.** Bumba is setting forth values by which his people should live. They should live in friendship and in peace, respecting one another and all of life. They should also appreciate being alive and the beauty of the universe.

THE QUARREL BETWEEN SAGBATA AND SOGBO (PAGE 518)

1. **Fon gods.** The Fon gods are like human beings in their thoughts, feelings, and behavior. Sagbata and Sogbo have the same problems in getting along with one another that many brothers and sisters do. They irritate one another by encroaching upon each other, and they argue incessantly. Then Sagbata removes everything that is his and stalks off. The fact that their mother comes to support Sogbo, who has remained at home, is also very human, as

is Sogbo's display of his power. Finally, once both brothers feel equally powerful, they become friends.

2. **Fon daily life.** Fon society as reflected in this myth combines practices from both the matriarchal and the patriarchal society. Mawu is the Great Goddess or Mother Goddess, and, in the matriarchal society, her youngest daughter would receive all the inheritance. However, as is customary in the patriarchal society, Mawu's oldest son receives that inheritance. The Fon were also known for prophecy, which is revealed by the arrival of two sky-beings who use their knowledge of past events to give advice about the future.

GASSIRE'S LUTE (PAGE 521)

1. **Gassire as hero.** It is important that Gassire is portrayed as a great hero because it puts his personality in perspective. He is the son of the king, the next in line for the throne, and his father obviously will not live that much longer. He is a great hero of the Fasa, and possibly he should be satisfied with the wealth, honor, and public acclaim that he has. However, he is extremely dissatisfied and unhappy with his situation.

2. **Gassire's choice.** To Gassire, fame is more important than anything else, including the welfare of his family and the welfare of his community (Wagadu). Therefore, he sacrifices the lives of his sons so that his lute will sing. His choice to play his lute also leads to his father's death and the fall of Wagadu.

3. **Sacrifice of sons.** Gassire sacrifices the lives of his sons to the lute by taking them with him into battle, where they are killed. Their blood falls upon his lute as he carries them back to Wagadu. The lute finally sings because enough family blood is absorbed into the wood so that the lute has a tale to sing—the tale of Gassire's heroism in battle and the death of his sons.

4. **Citizens of Wagadu.** The citizens of Wagadu are outraged by the battles Gassire initiates in order to gain fame, because their husbands and sons are also dying in these battles. Their choice is to let Gassire remain within the city and continue such wars or to banish him and risk being conquered by the Burdama. They banish Gassire, and they are conquered.

5. **Vanity.** Wagadu falls because of vanity for two reasons. First, Gassire's pride, evident in his need for greater fame, provokes the citizens of Wagadu to banish him. Second, the citizens of Wagadu think they can survive without Gassire. They mistakenly think that they are stronger than their enemy and that therefore they can relax their defense of the city.

6. **Character of Gassire.** Gassire is a courageous, strong, and skilled warrior who puts his own needs and desire for fame above everything else. As much as Gassire longs for the death of his father, he does not consider killing him, although many a son has killed his father in order to become king. However, Gassire has no qualms about killing seven of his eight sons in order to make

his lute sing. Students' opinions may vary, but although Gassire has performed many heroic deeds, he has caused so many unnecessary deaths that it is very difficult to admire him.

7. **Role of bloodshed.** It is possible that Gassire needs to shed blood in order to make the lute sing because this experience trains Gassire to be a more responsible king. Gassire needs to experience the deaths of his sons in order to understand, personally, one of the tragic aspects of war. The process of making the lute sing teaches Gassire humility through the experience of personal suffering.

It is also possible that the process of making the lute sing trains a bard to understand his subject from personal experience. Either way, the reader is struck with the extraordinarily high price that a person may have to pay in order to achieve immortal fame through heroic deeds.

Supplementary Suggestion
1. If your students have read *The Iliad,* you may want to compare Gassire and Achilles.

BAKARIDJAN KONE (PAGE 528)

1. **Birth and youth; tests; heroic stature.** Bakaridjan's birth is unusual in that it is the king, and not his father, who gives him his name. He develops a personality that reflects his status as a noble. Even though he is very poor, he possesses extraordinary self-confidence. His youth is unusual in that he passes the king's test that is devised to reveal who will be Segu's greatest hero, and he proves that he is a greater hero than any and all of the king's sons.

Bakaridjan's first test involves remaining silent and still while the king drives his spear through his foot as he mounts and dismounts his horse. This takes courage, determination, and endurance. This test also reveals Bakaridjan's attitude toward his king. Bakaridjan unquestioningly accepts the authority of Da Monzon, and he will do his best to perform whatever tasks his king demands of him.

Bakaridjan's second test involves enduring the three attempts of the king's sons to kill him. Once again, Bakaridjan displays courage, determination, and endurance. Moreover, his tolerance of the three beatings justifies his combat with Da Toma and his killing the king's oldest son. Bakaridjan's success in this single, hand-to-hand combat demands courage, strength, and skill.

2. **Tasks and benefit to society.** First, Bakaridjan attacks the Fula single-handedly and recovers the cattle of Segu that the Fula had stolen.

Bakaridjan then confronts Bilissi, the water-jinn, who is tyrannizing Segu. Because no one else has the courage, strength, or skill to combat him, Bilissi is free to get his own way with the people of Segu. Bakaridjan's confrontation results in Bilissi's fatal injury, and then Bakaridjan kills him.

Third, Bakaridjan captures the cattle of Samaniana, thereby giving his own people a breed of cattle that is superior to their own.

Meanwhile, throughout his adult life, Bakaridjan has continued to lead successful attacks against other city-states and kingdoms, capturing them in the name of Da Monzon, and thus enlarging Da Monzon's kingdom and his treasury.

3. **Rivalry among the three heroes.** The rivalry among the three heroes for Aminata's hand in marriage is particularly interesting because it reveals their society's attitudes toward its women, toward its heroes, and toward magic. First, in a society in which men have several wives, a woman can be so highly valued that three heroes will combat a fourth hero in order to win her as his wife.

Second, their society so values heroism as an end in itself that it makes life and death an entertainment. This society will risk the lives of its heroes just for the fun of seeing who the winner of a contest will be. Moreover, the contest reveals how fickle this society is toward its heroes, because the winner becomes Segu's greatest hero no matter how much or how little he has previously done for Segu. The important question appears to be, 'What have you done for us lately?'

Third, the belief in someone's ability to predict what is going to happen and the belief in magical protection is so strong that it determines the course of human behavior. Bakaridjan is "spooked" by the apparent power of his adversary. Even though Bakaridjan is supposedly Segu's greatest hero and, therefore, should be self-confident in meeting Dosoke Zan in single combat, his belief that he has lost his magical protection and his belief in Dosoke Zan's greater magical power leads him to reject the competition. Bakaridjan knows how fickle his society is toward its heroes. He knows that he will be regarded as a coward, despite all that he has done for his people. However, his fear of Dosoke Zan is so great that he accepts the consequences of cowardice in order to avoid accepting the risk of certain death.

This incident humanizes Bakaridjan because he exhibits fears and behavior that are characteristic of an ordinary person rather than a hero. It shows that the human personality is very complex. Bakaridjan can have different attitudes and behave differently under different circumstances and at different times in his life.

4. **Magic.** Three types of magic exist. First, particular people are able to predict future events based upon their interpretation of the Koran and their toss of kola nuts. The prophecy that Bakaridjan will be Segu's greatest hero causes the king always to view Bakaridjan as a threat to his own power. The prophecy with regard to Bakaridjan's combat with Bilissi saves Bakaridjan's life. He learn to avoid Bilissi's rope. Moreover, the contest between the rams accurately foreshadows the nature of their race, and it prepares Bakaridjan to deal with the dry well. The Aminata episode reveals the limits of a morike's ability to foretell the future, because two of the morikes do not know what will happen, and none of them appears to know that Dosoke Zan will take their protective charms from the heroes.

Second, people can gain magical protection that will save their lives. Morikes confer such protection upon the three heroes in the Aminata episode, but then Dosoke Zan steals it. The power of magical protection to provide the hero with actual or at least psychological security is evident in its absence, once Dosoke Zan has stolen it. Without his belief in the power of magic to protect his life, Bakaridjan does not possess the necessary self-confidence to fight Dosoke Zan. He will not fight a man whose magic is stronger than his own. In the case of Bilissi, the contest between the rams proved to him that his magic would be stronger than Bilissi's. Otherwise, it is possible that Bakaridjan would not have chosen to fight him either.

Third, people can gain magical power so that weapons will not hurt them. The water-jinn, Bilissi, possesses this power. Only wood can kill him. Dosoke Zan possesses this power as well.

Magic may be an attempt to account for the irrational, or the element of chance, or luck in life. It provides an explanation for why events turn out as they do. For example, in combat, it explains why some attacks succeed and others fail, and why one combatant dies and the other lives.

5. **Djeli's request and the Bambara hero.** At this time, a Bambara hero needs to prove his courage and skill repeatedly in order to maintain his stature in society. Therefore, the djeli is consciously doing Bakaridjan a favor by making a difficult request. He knows that the nobility will honor the request of the djeli in order to keep the djeli's good opinion, and the process of acquiring the cattle of Samaniana will bring Bakaridjan the fame that he needs in order to restore his heroic image. The nature of the djeli's request—the stealing of cattle from a neutral city-state—reveals that it is acceptable to attack a neutral country and lose human lives in order to gain fame and possessions. Apparently, fame is more important than peace, and war is an acceptable means to get whatever a king (or his djeli) wants.

6. **Da Monzon.** Da Monzon's personality makes him Bakaridjan's antagonist as well as his benefactor. Once Da Monzon hears the prophecy about Bakaridjan and learns Bakaridjan's identity, he never is comfortable with the hero's existence. Consequently, he encourages his sons to kill him, and when they are unsuccessful, he always hopes for another opportunity. Bakaridjan remains a thorn in his side, because the king knows that Bakaridjan possesses greater courage, strength, and skill than he himself does. Bakaridjan proves this to both of them when Bilissi comes to Segu City and terrorizes the people. At the end of the epic, when Simbalan foils Da Monzon's personal attempt to kill the hero, Da Monzon is forced to live with his fear, at least temporarily. He will always look for an opportunity to kill Bakaridjan, even if he has to find a way to kill Simbalan first in order to do it.

Da Monzon's personality humanizes him and reflects psychological realism. It is understandable for an autocrat to fear threats to his position and his power. He would therefore feel ambivalent about his greatest hero, who is best able both to defend his kingdom and to wrest it from him, and who has the affection of the people.

Da Monzon's personality also contributes to Bakaridjan's status because someone as powerful as a king is afraid of the country's hero, even when those who can discover the future make it clear to the king that Bakaridjan has no interest in becoming king, or anything other than what he already is.

7. **The ideal king: Da Monzon and Bassi.** The ideal king places the welfare of his people before his own wishes, and he thinks before he acts.

Da Monzon is probably viewed quite differently by different segments of society. If common people are in his army, they may resent having to risk their lives in order to enhance the prestige of their king. They know that, should they die, their wives and children would suffer economically. The nobility of Segu may welcome all the opportunities for heroism that Da Monzon provides. They may also profit from the wealth, in land, slaves, and treasure that their aggression provides whenever they are successful. For all those who are not the Bambara of Segu, Da Monzon is a tyrannical, blood-thirsty, and greedy king, who adds to his own empire and his own wealth by conquering the peoples of other kingdoms. The king whom Da Monzon defeats loses power, wealth, and human lives. The losing king must pay tribute to Da Monzon as proof of Da Monzon's authority over him, and the losing king undoubtedly views this payment as a form of extortion.

Bassi is depicted as an ideal king. Rather than fight Bakaridjan (and Da Monzon), he places his people and his cattle (a source of his country's wealth) safely behind the defensive walls of his city-state. He does not care whether or not others view him as a coward. He views it as his responsibility to be the protector of his people, and he knows that to lose to the Bambara of Segu is to lose freedom, life, and wealth.

8. **Simbalan Kone.** The characterization of Simbalan, like that of Da Monzon and Bakaridjan, contributes psychological realism and psychological complexity to the epic. From Simbalan's behavior, the reader gets some sense of what it is like to be the son of a great hero, particularly when that son wants to become a great hero himself.

Simbalan is his father's greatest advocate and supporter. He stands up to Da Monzon three times, first to get Da Monzon to recognize Bakaridjan as Segu's hero, and the other two times to save Bakaridjan's life (first, with regard to the paralysis Bilissi inflicted, and later, with regard to Da Monzon's plot).

Simbalan also acts so as to save his father's life in his father's conflict with the slave who is guarding the cattle of Samaniana. However, in his own mind in this instance, Simbalan would not only be saving his father's life, but he would also be a hero in his own right. Bakaridjan has a different point of view. In terms of the Bambara code of honor, Simbalan is usurping his father's prerogative and, therefore, he is overstepping his boundaries.

However, Simbalan apparently learns that, if he wishes to interfere in his father's life, it is best to continue to keep his plans to himself. Had he told Bakaridjan that he had learned of Da Monzon's plot, Bakaridjan probably would have forbidden him to interfere. Therefore, if he were to interfere, he would be showing disrespect to his father. As it is, Bakaridjan accepts Simbalan's intrusion, and Simbalan finally accomplishes what he had intended to accomplish in the earlier situation with the slave from Samaniana. He both saves his father's life and becomes a hero in his own right in the eyes of Da Monzon, who now fears him as well as his father.

Father and son appear to have an excellent relationship because they respect and appreciate each other. Bakaridjan's handling of Simbalan's intrusion into his conflict with the slave from Samaniana is appropriately controlled and instructive. Many another father might have responded more emotionally under equally disturbing circumstances. Moreover, Simbalan responds to Bakaridjan's response in an appropriately controlled manner, realizing the seriousness of his well-intentioned blunder, appreciating his father's reaction, and acknowledging the lesson that his father would teach him.

9. **Role of women.** Women play an interesting role in this epic, where the world is a man's world. For example, men have more than one wife, whereas women have only one husband. The warriors are men, not women. The djeli, the smiths, and the practitioners of magic are also men. However, although women have few noteworthy roles in the epic, two of the three women who do, possess the power to shape important events.

The Aminata episode involves the competition of three men for one woman. Moreover, society, speaking through the actions of the king's djeli, is delighted to have four heroes involved in combat in order to see who among them is the winner. Aminata, unlike Helen of Troy, does not have a face that will launch a thousand ships, but she possesses enough value in her society to launch the contest that ensues.

Da Monzon's wife is depicted as the woman who cannot keep her mouth shut. Fortunately for this stereotypical view of women, her husband could not keep his mouth shut either. If he had, she would have had no gossip to spread. However, it is also possible that Da Monzon's wife was not spreading gossip. The reader never knows whether Da Monzon's wife supports her husband in his plot against Bakaridjan's life. It is conceivable that she feels that he is being unjust toward Bakaridjan and that she tells her personal slave about the plot in the hope that the slave will speak to Simbalan.

Da Monzon's wife's favorite slave has, and wields, the verbal power to save Bakaridjan's life. Although she has no power in terms of the social structure of her society, she is free to confide her knowledge to Simbalan and to show him how to enter Da Monzon's private room.

10. **Slaves.** Slaves are at the bottom of the social ladder in Bambara society. Yet, many of them may have been nobles among their own people, and they are slaves only because they were captured in war. Consequently, they do not lack courage or intelligence just because of their social status.

Slaves may be very highly regarded by their masters, and they prove that they deserve the regard in which they are held. Da Monzon's wife clearly values her personal slave, and this woman has the courage to speak to and aid

Simbalan, thereby enabling him to save Bakaridjan's life. She appreciates the respect and kindness with which Simbalan has always treated her, and she does her best to repay him.

Bakaridjan's personal slave repays his own master's respect and kindness by creating and undertaking a dangerous mission. He exhibits creative intelligence and courage in his plot to disarm King Bassi of Samaniana, and he is successful in the dangerous role that he creates for himself. Finally, the slave whom King Bassi chooses to guard his kingdom's famous cattle is also one who possesses loyalty, courage, and determination. He fights the greatest hero of his time and place without flinching, treating his responsibility as an honor and trust to be guarded with his life.

11. **Bakaridjan's personality.** Bakaridjan is a hero who is human enough to be real. He is so self-confident as a youth that he comes before Da Monzon independently, rather than in the company of the slave who came for him. He also will not tolerate the king's belittling manner.

He is so courageous and loyal to his king that he tolerates the pain of the king's spear in his foot without a sign of discomfort. He is so clever and courageous that he captures Segu's cattle from the Fula by pretending that he is an entire army. He is so courageous that he confronts Bilissi even though the water-jinn possesses superhuman powers.

He is respectful of others, despite their lower social status. This is evident in his treatment of the blacksmith and in his treatment of his personal slave.

He is constantly loyal to Da Monzon, making no effort to usurp his position and power. His ambition is limited to being Segu's greatest hero.

He is generous in his aid, both financial and in terms of his personal help, to those who are less fortunate than he is. According to the epic, he supplies food to the poor and carries the heavy bundles of the weak.

12. **Master and victim of fame.** Bakaridjan becomes the master of his fame by using courage, strength, and skill to deal with his adversaries. As a youth, he obeys Da Monzon's wishes despite excruciating pain. Similarly, he tolerates the abuse of Da Monzon's sons until, at last, he must confront Prince Da Toma in battle. Then, Bakaridjan fights to win, and he emerges victorious. Bakaridjan is also master of his fame when the Fula steal the cattle of Segu, and Bakaridjan, alone among the warriors of Segu, uses his wits and rescues the cattle single-handedly. Bakaridjan is similarly the master of his fame in successful combat against a water-jinn who possesses superhuman powers and tyrannizes the people of Segu.

Students may disagree about whether Bakaridjan is the master of his fame or a coward when he decides not to fight Dosoke Zan. They should discuss whether a hero should feel compelled to do what he knows is wrong, either for himself or for his community, and how a hero should behave when a particular action is wrong for himself but helpful for his community. Bakaridjan does not consider how his behavior may affect Segu's safety. However, his refusal to fight Dosoke Zan may have public as well as personal consequences in that once Bakaridjan reveals himself to be a coward, his fear of death may encourage Segu's enemies to attack.

Bakaridjan is still the master of his fame when he refuses to fight Dosoke Zan because Bakaridjan acts despite his knowledge of the personal consequences. He realizes that Segu City offers a coward no refuge, even when that man has been a hero, and therefore he anticipates that the people of Segu will disapprove of his retreat. However, given that, thereafter, Bakaridjan must remain secretly confined within his home, it is possible that he does not anticipate his reaction to the ridicule he receives.

Bakaridjan becomes fame's victim in three ways. First, his community ridicules him for being unwilling to confront Dosoke Zan in battle because, in their view, a hero must always be courageous, no matter how foolish the situation. Therefore, Bakaridjan becomes hostage to public opinion. Student opinion may vary as to whether the community of Segu is correct in its view.

Second, Bakaridjan is fame's victim once he is willing to do whatever is necessary in order to regain fame in the opinion of the people of Segu. Thus he feels compelled to steal the cattle of Samaniana—and to initiate a battle with Samaniana's warriors—even though Samaniana is at peace with Segu, and King Bassi has no wish to confront Bakaridjan in battle. Students may disagree about whether Bakaridjan's behavior toward the people of Samaniana is heroic. They may sympathize with Bakaridjan's need to "save face," or they may consider it unheroic to provoke a battle in order to achieve private gain. It will be interesting to discuss the extent to which the leaders of nations find themselves compelled to engage other nations in war in order to "save face."

Third, Bakaridjan is fame's victim in that he must endure the fear and jealousy of others, such as Da Monzon and his sons, and live with the risk that one among his own people will murder him. In fact, without the help of Simbalan, Bakaridjan would have been killed by Da Monzon.

13. **Most appealing hero.** Student opinion will probably vary. Bakaridjan is very appealing because of his many accomplishments. His cowardice will appeal to some, who will like his human frailty. It will lead others to choose another hero because they do not think that a hero should ever be a coward, even when he believes that he is facing certain death.

Simbalan is very appealing because of his personality. He is always supportive of his father, and he treats an old slave-woman with kindness and respect. He always has the courage to confront the king, whatever the personal consequences.

Dosoke Zan is very appealing because he confronts what could be certain death with courage and honor. He questions prophecy and magic, even when they should inspire the fear in him that they inspire in Bakaridjan.

THE AMERICAS

THE CREATION (PAGE 570)

1. **Stone people.** Students' opinions may vary. The fact that Viracocha causes his stone people to sink beneath the earth before they reappear may reflect a fusion of religious ideas: the idea of one creator and the idea of natural phenomena producing life. Having people born from rocks, rivers, mountains, and caves would cause people to worship those forms of nature.

2. **Viracocha's disappearance.** Viracocha disappears in the way he does in order to enhance his image. He is last seen doing what no human being can do. Seeing a creator-god perform a miraculous deed is more impressive than simply seeing him disappear.

THE CHILDREN OF THE SUN (PAGE 574)

1. **Opening descriptions.** If we go back far enough in the history of human beings, people originally lived as the Inca describe them at the beginning of this myth. However, the Inca possessed no history of the peoples who preceded them. Their own history was transmitted through an established oral tradition. Therefore, as they look back to their own beginnings, their difference from the peoples they lived among was more a difference of attitude than a difference of technology.

2. **Character of Sun.** It is Sun who cares about people because the sun permits life to exist on earth. The Inca possibly could have chosen water as the caring element in nature, or even air.

3. **Fertility.** Sun claims responsibility for the fertility of the soil because the Inca realized the connection between the sun and the growth of plants. They also realized the importance of water, but they did not realize that the sun did not control the rain.

4. **Purpose of myth.** This myth tells, first, how the Inca came to settle in the Cuzco valley, and second, how the Inca leaders created the Inca people and made them civilized by giving them an advanced technology.

WANADI, THE CREATOR (PAGE 578)

1. **Wanadi and Odosha and the Yekuhana universe.** Wanadi and Odosha reveal a universe in which the good divinity must always confront evil in his universe. However, that evil exists in tangible form in the being of Odosha, who has the power to influence human beings to behave in evil ways. Wanadi is all good. However he is not all powerful. Therefore, evil continues to exist in the universe.

2. **How Odosha exerts power over Wanadi.** Odosha exerts power over Wanadi indirectly by influencing human beings to choose evil behavior instead of good behavior. Because Odosha's suggestions usually bring immediate gain or pleasure, the human beings to whom he whispers usually listen to him and follow his suggestions.

   In reality, Odosha exists as an internal, rather than an external force. He is that part of each individual that wants to do what the individual knows is ethically wrong.

3. **Why Wanadi and Odosha never conquer each other.** The fact that Wanadi and Odosha never succeed in conquering each other in the myth explains the fact that the universe always contains both good and evil. However, the myth reflects reality in that evil often appears to conquer good, such as when people suffer from illness, poverty, and war.

4. **Hope for the Yekuhana people.** Those human beings who refuse to listen to Odosha's evil whisperings and who therefore resist any inclination to act in evil ways will, after their death, be permitted to enter Sky, the home of Wanadi and the good Sky People. There, they will spend eternity in a joyful land of plenty and peace.

   Moreover, the myth assumes that a time will come when evil will disappear, Odosha will die, and a new earth will replace the present one. Then, all will return to the utopia of the universe as it existed in the beginning.

5. **Why Wanadi sends spirit doubles.** Wanadi's spirit doubles reflect a view of the universe in which every living being has the form, speech, and often the name of its master in the sky. The master in the sky, whether Wanadi or one of the other sky people, remains a permanent fixture. In contrast, like everything else on earth, the spirit messengers come and go. The beings that live on earth are only copies of their master. Wanadi protects himself by being able to separate his spirit from its form, as he does at the end of the myth. This separation of the spirit protects it and makes it invulnerable, despite whatever may befall the body that houses it.

6. **Ability of people and animals to change their form.** The ability of people and animals to change their form symbolizes an inscrutable and magical universe in which everything may, in reality, be different from what it appears to be. Therefore, human beings are very vulnerable, and they respond to their environment with fear, caution, and respect. The belief in powers of transformation is consistent with a forest environment, where it is dark, where trees and a thick undergrowth conceal people and animals, and where the light that flickers through the trees makes vision unclear.

THE CREATION (PAGE 595)

1. **Why several races.** The Mayan Creators are not more perfect than human beings. They are not able to create the race of human beings they want because they do not know in advance how each race will turn out. Not only

can they not anticipate what problems the materials they have chosen will cause, but they cannot make the human beings they create obey their wishes. Human beings continue to have independence from the Mayan gods; they are not puppets.

2. **Why races destroyed or changed.** The Creators destroy the race of wood because the creatures lack intelligence and emotions. Therefore, they cannot praise and love their creators. On the other hand, the race of cornmeal is too intelligent and wise. They praise their creators and love them, but the Creators now feel inferior to the people they have created. Consequently, they modify the cornmeal race by removing enough of their intelligence so that the Creators are more intelligent than their creation. This reveals that the Mayan gods are superior to human beings and wish to be separated from them. Human beings have their proper place, as creations that are inferior to those who created them.

THE CREATION CYCLE (PAGE 600)

1. **Succession of worlds.** Students' opinions may vary. One implication is that our fifth world will be destroyed as the gods destroyed the other four worlds unless human beings behave properly toward one another and the gods. Consequently, this myth is designed to teach proper behavior.

2. **Importance of ugly god.** The fact that an ugly, sore-infested god makes the supreme sacrifice and that he is honored for doing so teaches that even the worst appearing and least significant of beings can perform deeds of great value in life.

3. **Human sacrifice.** Human beings are sacrificed to appease the earth goddess's thirst for blood and to assure fertility. The people who created this myth and the religious practices that it explains felt that since the earth was feeding human beings, it would have to feed on human beings in return. They could have found a reason why the earth would have been satisfied with the blood of animals or simply prayers.

4. **Aspects of life.** These four creation myths explain the importance of blood sacrifice and music in Aztec life. Gods must sacrifice their lives in order for the sun to shine. Quetzalcoatl sacrifices his blood in order to fashion human beings. Human beings sacrifice other human beings in order to motivate the earth to provide them with food.

5. **Quetzalcoatl.** Based upon these myths, Quetzalcoatl makes the universe operate in such a way that life can exist on earth. In the third myth, he creates human beings. He is a very caring, selfless creator, carefully searching for the best food for them and using his own blood to fashion them. He is also clever in that he devises a scheme whereby he can steal the corn he wants from the ants. In the second and fourth myths, Quetzalcoatl works together with Tezcatlipoca as two human beings would work together to achieve a goal. Together they create the earth and fill it with music.

QUETZALCOATL (PAGE 609)

1. **Quetzalcoatl's birth.** Quetzalcoatl's birth is unusual in that a feather from the sun impregnates his mother. Quetzalcoatl grows to the size of a nine year old within a few days of his birth. His birth enhances his heroic image because it sets him apart at once as a most remarkable being.

2. **Quetzalcoatl's heroic tasks.** Quetzalcoatl helps recover his father's body when the stars kill him, thereby restoring the sun to the universe. For the survival of life on earth, no task would be more important than that one. He also teaches the people how to raise corn and cotton, so that they will be well fed and clothed. He teaches them to weave cloth, to write and paint, to dance, and to create objects made of gold, jade, feathers, wood, and stone. Being the model of proper behavior, he respects all forms of life.

3. **Enemies.** Students' opinions may vary. It is natural for some human beings to want power enough to try to gain it whatever way they can. When election is available, they run for office. Otherwise, some among them may be motivated to kill a ruler in order to take his place. Some are satisfied to be certain that no one is more powerful than they are. If they cannot be what they want to be, they try to make it difficult for other people to be successful. However, these people are the rare few. Most people are content to let other people be powerful as long as they have enough to be content with their own lives.

4. **Quetzalcoatl and Tezcatlipoca.** These characters are alike in that they are both very intelligent beings and creator-gods. However, Tezcatlipoca is more intelligent than Quetzalcoatl, and he has a cruel nature as well as a kind one. He is also more ambitious. Since he cannot be as good as Quetzalcoatl, who has no cruelty in his inner nature, Tezcatlipoca sets out to destroy Quetzalcoatl. He succeeds because he is clever enough to know where Quetzalcoatl's vulnerable spots are.

5. **Quetzalcoatl's temptations.** Tezcatlipoca can conquer Quetzalcoatl because he understands how insecure each person basically is, no matter how successful he or she appears to be to everyone else. Tezcatlipoca receives his own strength and power from his success in preying upon the inherent weaknesses of others; he is intelligent enough to be able to cause the strongest of human beings to doubt themselves.

   Because Quetzalcoatl cannot recognize and accept his own capacity to be vain and immoral, he cannot protect himself against such behavior. Evil magicians cannot tempt him to perform human sacrifices, but he is sensitive to his own physical appearance and wants people to think only the best of him. Once Tezcatlipoca makes him look in a mirror, Quetzalcoatl fears that his people will destroy him because he is so ugly. In order to prove how courageous he is, Quetzalcoatl tastes the drink Tezcatlipoca offers him. He finds the taste so appealing that he becomes drunk on it, not having the self-confidence to ignore Tezcatlipoca's accusations of cowardice.

6. **Tezcatlipoca's strength.** Tezcatlipoca conquers Quetzalcoatl by destroying his self-confidence and pride. Quetzalcoatl continues to rule, but self-consciously and without pride in himself.

7. **Destruction of Quetzalcoatl.** Tezcatlipoca can be certain that he has destroyed Quetzalcoatl because he knows that he has proved Quetzalcoatl to be vulnerable and fallible, when Quetzalcoatl had to feel that he was perfect.

8. **Quetzalcoatl as hero.** Students' opinions may vary. On the one hand, Quetzalcoatl's behavior simply proves that he is human. Many deeds testify to his greatness, and many more may add to his reputation. He remains a good human being, one who is sensitive to the needs of others. On the other hand, Quetzalcoatl's inability to recognize the potential for evil in himself made it easy for him to commit evil deeds. Heroes will be greater if they possess greater self-knowledge, for that knowledge will give them greater control over their own behavior.

9. **Why Tezcatlipoca destroys people.** Tezcatlipoca decides to destroy Quetzalcoatl's people for a number of reasons. First, he enhances his own self-esteem by exerting his power over others. Second, he proves to Quetzalcoatl how powerful he is. Third, he destroys not only his rival, but his rival's kingdom, intending to leave him with nothing.

   Tezcatlipoca possesses both the wisdom to realize the value of intelligence and the experience to know that people let their emotions rather than their intelligence determine their behavior. He is able to succeed with his clever schemes because they are designed to appeal to emotions rather than to the intellect. The people are so gullible that they do not realize that Tezcatlipoca is manipulating them just as he is manipulating the puppet of Quetzalcoatl. They react to the emotional appeal of Tezcatlipoca's schemes, and they do not look before they leap.

10. **Good versus self-destructive qualities.** Tezcatlipoca proves that unless people use their intelligence and think critically before they act, they risk the possibility of destroying themselves. When people rush blindly off to war, or dance themselves into a frenzy, or eat whatever is appealing just because it is tantalizing, their behavior will destroy them. Tezcatlipoca proves that too much of any good thing is evil.

11. **Irony.** Ironically, Tezcatlipoca turns many of the gifts Quetzalcoatl had given his people into disasters. Their passionate love of music kills them. Their excessive patriotism kills them. Their great hunger for tasty food (corn) kills them.

12. **Why creators of myth allow destruction.** Students' opinions may vary. Possibly the purpose of the myth is to show how vulnerable good is to the forces of evil. Certainly, the power of evil in the myth is terrifying. The myth demands that both leaders and common people look within themselves, acknowledge their weaknesses, and use that knowledge to control the direction of their lives. If they do not, they are not human beings; they are puppets.

13. **Why Quetzalcoatl leaves country a wasteland.** Students' opinions may vary. Possibly Quetzalcoatl is angry with his people for being weak and wishes to punish those among them who are still alive. Possibly he wishes to leave Tezcatlipoca with a poor and barren land to rule. However, Quetzalcoatl is not permitted to be totally destructive. Demons force him to leave behind the skills and wealth that he still possesses, so that others can profit from these great gifts.

14. **Would Quetzalcoatl be welcomed back.** The Aztec emperor would have welcomed Quetzalcoatl back to Mexico because he valued the leader's great qualities and accepted his weaknesses.

15. **Quetzalcoatl versus Tezcatlipoca.** Students' opinions will vary. The choice is between two extraordinary beings, both of whom gave precious gifts to human beings. Students may need to be reminded that it was Tezcatlipoca who gave human beings intelligence. It becomes more understandable then that he punished them when they did not use it.

THE EMERGENCE (PAGE 615)

1. **Civilization process.** The depiction of a creative process in which living creatures become more complex and civilized as they move from one world to another has the appeal of optimism. The person who thinks that life in the world is constantly improving is a happy one.

2. **Human beings and animals.** The myth reveals that the Navajo perceive a close relationship between human beings and animals. Early in their history, all living creatures had teeth, claws, feet, and wings, and they spoke a common language. Together they survived the flood. The feeling of kinship still exists.

LODGE-BOY AND THROWN-AWAY (PAGE 622)

1. **Courage and skill.** The twins are courageous in that they approach each villain without fear. They are skillful in that they can move very quietly, and they have clever minds. They kill the otter by throwing hot rocks into its mouth. They deliver just punishments by killing some villains using the villains' own techniques. For example, the boys boil the woman who boils people in her own pot; they cause the man who pushes people over the cliff to fall over the cliff himself; and they burn the man who burns people with his own flaming moccasins.

2. **How twins help community.** The twins help their community by killing people and monsters who prey upon innocent passers-by. Thereafter, people can travel as they choose in safety.

3. **Heroic children.** The fact that the heroes are children adds to the appeal of the myth. Possibly this myth was told to children, because children would be

more interested in children than in adults. Children are often likely to be more adventurous and creative than ordinary adults. The disadvantage of child heroes is that they are smaller and not as strong as adults. That is why they have to catch the villains when they are asleep, or they have to pit their clever intelligence against the brute strength of the villains.

THE WOMAN WHO FELL FROM THE SKY (PAGE 625)

1. **Female versus male divinities.** The creation myth reflects the organization of Iroquois matriarchal society, in which females own the land and farm it, while males are hunters. Each divinity creates the occupation of the people of her or his sex.

2. **Evil and Good Twin.** Evil Twin exists because his actions account for all of the troubles that human beings endure in the world. The brothers are twins because they represent a view of the universe in which life began with a balance between the forces of good and evil. The twins also represent, in an externalized form, the capacity of each individual to be both good and evil.

3. **Why Good Twin kills Evil Twin.** The actions of Good Twin and Evil Twin create what is good and bad in the universe. Their confrontation, in which Good Twin kills Evil Twin and then leaves the earth, causes the universe to remain forever as they have created it. Consequently, the Iroquois view the universe as the source of both good and evil, and they view the situation as getting neither better nor worse at any time in the future.

Supplementary Question

1. If your students have read either or both of the following myths, have them consider how the Iroquois view of the universe differs from the views expressed in the Greek "The Ages of Man" and the Indian "The Creation, Death, and Rebirth of the Universe."

RAVEN AND THE SOURCES OF LIGHT (PAGE 634)

1. **Daily life.** This myth reveals that the Haida, Tlingit, and Tsimshian peoples lived by fishing. The family was important, as is clear from the way the grandfather treats his grandson with great love.

2. **Character of Raven.** Raven is very clever and mischievous. Most students would probably enjoy having him as a friend because being with him would be interesting, exciting, and unpredictable. Undoubtedly, Raven would get into a lot of trouble, but just as certainly he would find a creative way to escape.

3. **Values.** The role of Raven reveals a culture in which the people feel a kinship with animals. Raven's personality indicates that the people value a sense of humor. They enjoy hearing about the adventures of an animal hero who is intelligent and clever enough to trick even the chief of the tribe.

SEDNA (PAGE 637)

1. **Character of Sedna.** Students' responses may vary. Possible answers may include: rebellious: Sedna chooses to disobey the dictates of her society and instead chooses her own marriage partner; persevering: Sedna hangs on to her father's boat despite the injuries she receives; vengeful: Sedna punishes her father for his treatment of her.

2. **Death of bird-man.** Students may take opposite points of view on this question. Some may believe Sedna's father is justified in killing the bird-man because the bird-man wooed his daughter under false pretenses and then mistreated her. Others may feel Sedna's father is not justified because Sedna married the bird-man despite all of her father's warnings. Consequently, Sedna is responsible for her own fate.

3. **Death of Sedna.** Students' opinions may vary. Most students will probably think that a father is never justified in killing his child. Some may think Sedna's father is not justified in killing Sedna because he, and not Sedna, killed Sedna's husband. Sedna did not even ask him to do it. Some students are likely to think that the father acted out of terror and that his actions are therefore excusable; moreover, it was Sedna's unwise marriage that put him into this precarious position.

4. **Seabirds' punishment of Sedna.** Students may disagree as to whether the seabirds are justified in punishing Sedna for her husband's death. Some may believe Sedna is responsible in that it is her unhappiness that leads her father to kill her husband and she does not protest the crime. However, from the seabirds' point of view, Sedna was well housed, well fed, and well loved. They would not understand her dissatisfaction and her unhappiness. Moreover, they would view her father as her agent and assume that he had simply carried out her wishes.

5. **Culture.** Sedna's character both reveals and represents the harsh, unpredictable nature of the environment in which the Inuit live. The sea, on which the people depend for their survival, is both a friend and an enemy. Sea animals are a necessary source of food, and the sea may or may not supply enough food. Moreover, the sea may permit the Inuit people to hunt its waters in safety, or it may destroy them. Consequently, through worship and ritual, the Inuit people try to placate Sedna, thereby hoping to survive.

    The myth also reinforces cultural values about the expected behavior of females in their society. The female should not be independent but should listen to the male patriarch and marry within the Inuit culture. This cultural value assures the continuity of the Inuit community and prolongs the life of the people as a whole. That this is an important message of the myth is supported by the idea that the myth continues to be a vital part of the religious life of modern Inuit communities.

CAUGHT BY A HAIR-STRING (PAGE 643)

1. **Description of hero.** The hero of this myth is always described as a lazy and unattractive-looking young man in order to depict him as an outsider in his community, where he is viewed with humor. The description is actually ironic in that the hero industriously works at becoming a man of power in his community.

2. **Hero and chief's son.** The significance of the relationship between the chief's son and the hero is their need for one another. Their relationship reveals the importance of companionship, friendship, and mentors.

3. **Role of forest.** The forest symbolizes spiritual isolation. It can be real, or it can represent the soul or the subconscious of an individual. Either way, it is the environment in which dreams about spiritual power can occur.

4. **Acquiring power.** In order to be able to acquire power in Micmac society, one must value power in those who possess it, one must be willing to learn about power from those who would teach it, and one must have spiritually significant dreams.

5. **Need for power.** The need for spiritual power reveals that the Micmac people live in a frightening environment that always threatens to overpower them. In order to survive, they need power or need to associate with one who has power because wild animals, lack of food, illness, and human enemies are all potentially fatal threats.

6. **Lesson of myth.** A person who hears this myth might gain a greater appreciation of the value of friendship, with its companionship, communication, and reciprocal support. Another lesson is that those who appear to be less valuable can prove most valuable to the community.

7. **Contemporary forms of power.** Students' opinions may vary. Two possibilities are: challenging careers, which are obtained through the successful pursuit of the appropriate education; and the ability to influence the laws of our society, which is accomplished by voting, by becoming a community leader, or by becoming an elected representative of the people at the local, state, or national level of government.